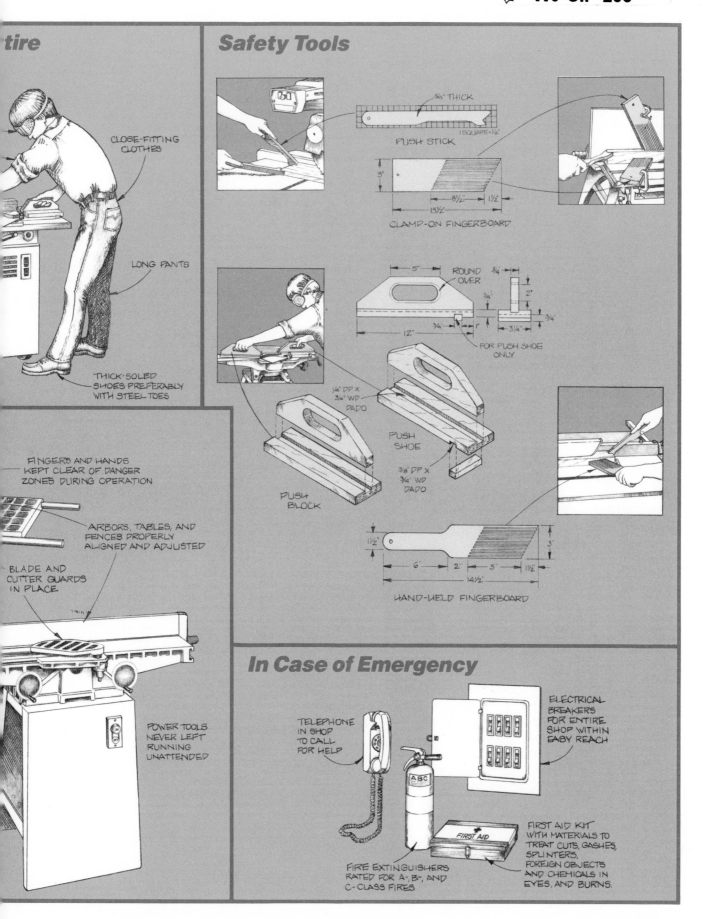

tire

Safety Tools

CLOSE-FITTING CLOTHES

LONG PANTS

THICK-SOLED SHOES PREFERABLY WITH STEEL TOES

¾" THICK

1 SQUARE = ½"

PUSH STICK

3"

8½"

1½"

13½"

CLAMP-ON FINGERBOARD

5"

ROUND OVER

¾"

¾"

2"

¾"

12"

¾"

1"

3¼"

FOR PUSH SHOE ONLY

¼" DP X ¾" WD DADO

PUSH SHOE

⅜" DP X ¾" WD DADO

PUSH BLOCK

1½"

3"

6"

2"

5"

1½"

14½"

HAND-HELD FINGERBOARD

FINGERS AND HANDS KEPT CLEAR OF DANGER ZONES DURING OPERATION

ARBORS, TABLES, AND FENCES PROPERLY ALIGNED AND ADJUSTED

BLADE AND CUTTER GUARDS IN PLACE

POWER TOOLS NEVER LEFT RUNNING UNATTENDED

In Case of Emergency

ELECTRICAL BREAKERS FOR ENTIRE SHOP WITHIN EASY REACH

TELEPHONE IN SHOP TO CALL FOR HELP

ABC

FIRST AID

FIRE EXTINGUISHERS RATED FOR A-, B-, AND C- CLASS FIRES

FIRST AID KIT WITH MATERIALS TO TREAT CUTS, GASHES, SPLINTERS, FOREIGN OBJECTS AND CHEMICALS IN EYES, AND BURNS.

·BUILD·IT·BETTER·YOURSELF·
WOODWORKING PROJECTS

Shelving and Storage

Collected and Written
by Nick Engler

Rodale Press
Emmaus, Pennsylvania

Printed in the United States of America on acid-free paper containing a high percentage of recycled fiber.

Series Editor: William H. Hylton
Managing Editor/Author: Nick Engler
Copy Editor: Kate Armpriester
Graphic Designer: Linda Watts
Graphic Artist: Christine Vogel
Draftpersons: Mary Jane Favorite
            Chris Walendzak
Photography: Karen Callahan
Illustrations by O'Neil & Associates, Dayton, Ohio
Produced by Bookworks, Inc., West Milton, Ohio

Library of Congress Cataloging-in-Publication Data

Engler, Nick.
    Shelving and storage/collected and written by Nick
    Engler. p. cm. — (Build-it-better-yourself wood-
    working projects)
    ISBN: 0-87857-789-0
    1. Cabinet-work.   2. Shelving (Furniture)
    3. Storage in the home.
I. Title.   II. Series.
TT197.E54   1988
684.1′6—dc19   88-26347
    4   6   8   10   9   7   5   3   hardcover

Contents

Order from Chaos: An Introduction to Storage

Storage is our way of bringing some sense of order to all the things that clutter up our lives. Living in a consumer society, we accumulate stuff like pack rats. Books, tools, records, videotapes, kitchen utensils, clothes — the list is endless. Only by arranging these things so that they're accessible when we need them, but out of the way when we don't — in other words, *storing* them — can we keep from being overwhelmed by our own possessions.

The key to building a workable storage system is good organization. There are many clever storage projects in this book, but they won't do you a bit of good if you aren't properly organized. You must know *what* you've got and *where* you want to keep it before you build something to keep it in.

Some possessions are simple to organize. Silverware, for example, can be divided up into knives, forks, and spoons. You keep your silverware near the sink (where you wash it) or near the table (where you use it). But it's not quite as easy when you try to organize all your kitchen utensils. Where do you keep the turkey baster that you use only once a year? Did you even know you had a turkey baster?

To tackle those truly monumental storage nightmares, you have to think through the problem logically. Here are a few suggestions to help you arrive at an organized solution.

Knowing What You've Got... Taking Inventory

Even if you think you know what you've got, make a list of the things you want to organize. The act of listing them will force you to think about all your possessions that fit into the same category. Often, things will pop into mind that you might not have remembered otherwise. This doesn't mean that you should list every videotape or every jar of spices. But you should write down how many tapes or spice jars you have, so you'll know how much storage space you need for them.

As you make your list, divide the items into these four categories:

Things you use often — These are the things that you and your family use day-to-day. They might include eating and cooking utensils, laundry supplies, reference books, financial records, favorite toys, and clothing.

Things you use occasionally — Some of your possessions are an important part of your life, but only for part of the year or on certain occasions. Some of these are seasonal items such as snow shovels, beach towels, summer and winter clothing, air conditioners, and holiday decorations. This category might also include a slide projector, photo albums, sewing supplies, and certain tools that you only use once in a while.

Things you (almost) never use — There may be some items on your list that prompt you to wonder why you keep them around. They include equipment and supplies for activities that you or your family have long since lost interest in. There also may be baby furniture, gifts from in-laws, and broken items awaiting repair. Hint: These are all good candidates for a garage sale. You can solve the problem of where to store that broken rocker by making it someone else's.

Things you never use but can't part with — Most often, these include keepsakes and collections — seashells, antique tools, pottery, and so on. The items in the other categories may be useful and keep your life going, but these are the items that give your life meaning. They should play an important part in your storage plan.

Deciding Where to Keep It... Designing a Storage System

Once you know what you've got, the next step is to decide where to keep it. This question of "where" is a bigger question than you might first think. When you design a storage project, there are several different issues that you must consider:

Accessibility — When you store the items, how close do you want them to where they are actually used? The things in the first category — things you use often — generally have to be close at hand. But you probably won't be able to afford that luxury for everything on your list. Hint: Seasonal items can "swap places" if you design your storage projects accordingly. For example, a picnic cooler that you keep in the front of a closet during the summer might be replaced by skis and snow boots when winter comes.

Open or closed storage — Sometimes, you'll want to see the things you have stored, either to show them off or so you can get at them more easily. Other times, you'll want to hide the clutter. Shelves are the most common form of open storage; cabinets and drawers are the most common closed storage. In rare instances, you may decide on "open-but-closed" storage — storage units with glass doors or panels that will protect the things stored in them, but keep them in full view.

Dimensions — There are two sets of dimensions that you must take into account as you design the project. First of all, what are the dimensions of the items that you want to store? Second, what are the dimensions of the space that the completed storage unit will occupy? The first set of dimensions will determine the sizes of drawers and cabinets, the width and spacing of shelves and partitions. The second set will determine the overall size of the project.

Human engineering — The human body and how it works affect the design of a storage project in many different ways, some of them obvious, others more subtle. Usually, the most important human factor is *reach* — how far you can comfortably stretch in order to retrieve something from a shelf or cabinet. This is why most shelving units and cabinets are under 78″ tall and 24″ deep. That's about as far as the arms of an average-sized adult will reach.

In some projects, you have to consider other parts of the body. For example, when making shadowboxes for small objects, you have to design them around the size of your fingers. Some of the objects you have to store in the boxes may be smaller than your fingers, but if you can't reach into the compartments, how will you ever get those things in or out?

You may also want to personalize a storage unit for the people who will use it. Children do not have the reach of an adult, so projects like blanket chests and closet organizers may have to be scaled down to their size. Or you may have to adapt a project to compensate for the physical restrictions of a handicapped or elderly person.

Adapting Our Plans to Your Needs

With all of these separate considerations, it's likely that you will have to modify the projects in this book to suit yourself. For this reason, we have made them to be easily adapted. The slide-out bins, for example, can be made larger or smaller to fit your cabinets. When making the adjustable bookcase, you can choose among several different types of hardware to support the shelves. There are different closet organizer units you can insert in your closet, depending on what you want to store. By using different molding or fretwork, you can change the style of the wall system to match your decor without changing the basic construction. With each project, we've included suggestions for changing the dimensions, hardware, components, or style with the instructions.

As you page through this book looking for storage ideas, remember that all of the project designs are flexible. No matter how you answer the questions of *what* and *where,* they offer potential solutions to your storage problems.

There are three types of storage. The adjustable shelving unit is an example of open storage. The hanging ventilated cabinet provides closed storage. The glass-front wall cabinet falls somewhere in between; it's open-but-closed storage.

Wall Units

One of the most useful — and versatile — storage projects is the "wall unit." This stand-alone piece is a combination of a cabinet (below), shelves (above), and a counter or workspace (in the middle). Each unit reaches from the floor almost to the ceiling. Two or more wall units are often arranged next to one another, covering the entire wall — hence the strange name.

Wall units are traditionally used in dens and living rooms, but they may also be placed in kitchens, dining rooms, even bedrooms — anywhere you need to store things. They can be adapted to hold books, collectibles, audio and video equipment, foodstuffs, cooking utensils, dishes and silverware, linens and clothing — almost anything. They offer as much storage space as many built-ins, but because they are *movable,* they are more flexible. They can be rearranged as your storage needs change.

These projects are time-consuming to make, mainly because they are so large. They are not, however, particularly difficult to build. None of the joints or assemblies require any special skills or tools. With a little patience and persistence, you can build an elegant set of wall units in a modest workshop.

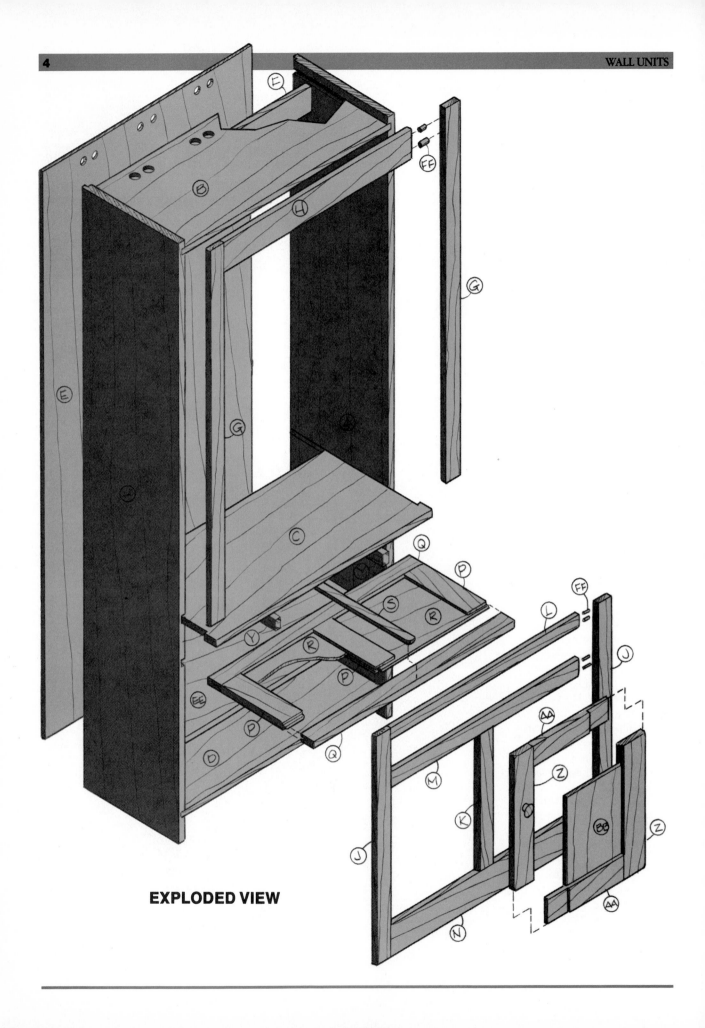

EXPLODED VIEW

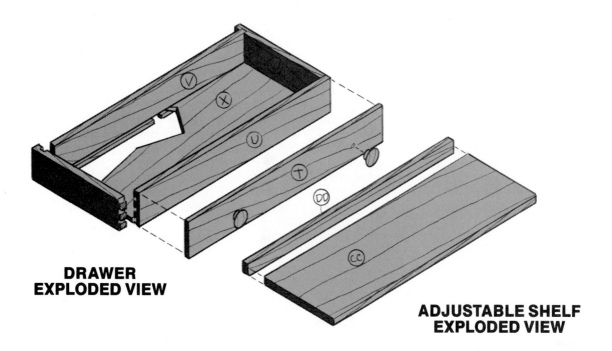

**DRAWER
EXPLODED VIEW**

**ADJUSTABLE SHELF
EXPLODED VIEW**

Materials List

FINISHED DIMENSIONS

PARTS

A.	Sides (2)	¾" x 14¼" x 78"
B.	Top	¾" x 14¼" x 33¼"
C.	Counter	¾" x 15⅝" x 34"
D.	Bottom	¾" x 13⅞" x 33¼"
E.	Back	⅜" x 33¼" x 72⅝"
F.	Light baffle	¾" x 3" x 32½"
G.	Top face frame stiles (2)	¾" x 2" x 48"
H.	Top face frame rail	¾" x 4" x 30"
J.	Bottom face frame outside stiles (2)	¾" x 2" x 29¼"
K.	Bottom face frame middle stile	¾" x 2" x 18"
L.	Bottom face frame top rail	¾" x 1¼" x 30"
M.	Bottom face frame middle rail	¾" x 2" x 30"
N.	Bottom face frame bottom rail	¾" x 4" x 30"
P.	Web-frame stiles (3)	¾" x 3" x 10⅝"
Q.	Web-frame rails (2)	¾" x 2" x 33¼"

R.	Dust shields (2)	¼" x 10⅝" x 12⅞"
S.	Drawer guide	¼" x 1" x 13⅞"
T.	Drawer face	⅜" x 4⅝" x 30⅝"
U.	Drawer front	¾" x 3⅞" x 29⅞"
V.	Drawer back	¾" x 3⅞" x 29⅛"
W.	Drawer sides (2)	¾" x 3⅞" x 14"*
X.	Drawer bottom	¼" x 12⅞" x 29⅛"
Y.	Kickers (2)	¾" x 1¼" x 13⅞"
Z.	Door stiles (4)	¾" x 3" x 18⅝"
AA.	Door rails (4)	¾" x 3" x 14⅝"
BB.	Door panels (2)	⅜" x 9⅛" x 13⅛"
CC.	Top adjustable shelves (2-3)	¾" x 11" x 32⅜"
DD.	Backstops (2-3)	¾" x 1½" x 32⅜"
EE.	Bottom adjustable shelf	¾" x 13¾" x 32⅜"
FF.	Dowels (20)	⅜" dia. x 2"

* This dimension may change slightly, depending on the joinery used to attach the drawer sides to the drawer front.

HARDWARE

#10 x 1¼" Flathead wood screws (24-36)
1" Brads (24-36)
Drawer pulls and mounting screws (2)
Door pulls and mounting screws (2)
Door catches (2)
Semi-concealed offset hinges and mounting screws (2 pairs)
Tube-style cabinet lights (3)
6-amp Toggle switch
Pin-style shelf supports (12-16)

1

Make any necessary changes in the size or design of the wall units. As designed, these units are 34″ wide, 78″ tall, and 15″ deep. Depending on the space in your home, you may want to change the size slightly. If you do change the overall dimensions, you obviously will have to adjust the dimensions of the individual parts.

You may want to change the style to match your decor. As shown, the units have a simple Shaker look. This will blend with both country and contemporary design. To make the units more formal, there are several things you can do:

- Add moldings or trim to the top and the bottom of the case.
- Substitute raised panels for the flat panels in the doors.
- Cut shapes in the top face frame to add fancy fretwork around the upper cabinet opening.
- Use decorative brasses instead of simple wooden pulls.

To see how these additions will look, trace a copy of the *Front View.* Sketch the moldings, trim, etc., on the drawing until you get the look you're after. Then make the appropriate amendments to the Materials List.

2

Cut all parts to size. If you build this project from solid wood, you will need approximately 50 board feet of cabinet-grade lumber, 10 board feet of utility lumber, a full sheet (4′ x 8′) of ⅜″ cabinet-grade plywood, and a half sheet (4′ x 4′) of ¼″ utility plywood for each wall unit. Use the cabinet-grade lumber and plywood for the parts that show, such as the sides, shelves, and back. Make those that don't show, such as the web frame pieces, from utility wood and plywood.

You can cut down on some of the solid cabinet-grade lumber you need by substituting ¾″ cabinet-grade plywood for the larger pieces — the sides, top, bottom, counter, and shelves. You won't necessarily save money, but you will save time and avoid worry. You don't have to dress the lumber or glue up boards to make these wide pieces. You won't have to worry that they'll cup or warp as time goes by. But you will have to edge the front of the counter and the shelves with strips of solid wood to hide the plies. If you use plywood for these parts, you'll need 1½ sheets and just 20 board feet of solid lumber.

Note: You must make *all* the larger parts from plywood or *all* from solid wood. Don't mix plywood and solid wood, or the case may break when the solid wood expands and contracts, and the plywood doesn't.

Once you have gathered the parts you need, cut all the parts to the sizes shown on the Materials List. Before you cut, however, make sure that your saw is in proper alignment. This is a large project, and even a small deviation off square can throw the case out of kilter when it's assembled.

3

Cut the joinery in the sides and top. The parts of the case are joined with dadoes and rabbets. Cut the rabbets first: Rout ⅜″-wide, ⅜″-deep rabbets in the back edges of the sides and the top. Then rout ¾″-wide, ⅜″ deep dadoes in the sides, where shown in the *Side Layout.* To make sure that both sides are routed exactly the same, clamp them front edge to front edge so that you can rout two dadoes at once — one in each piece. Lay a straightedge across *both* pieces to guide the router, and secure the straightedge to the sides. (See Figure 1.) Make each set of dadoes in several passes, cutting ⅛″ deeper with each pass.

1/Clamp a straightedge across both sides. This will serve as a guide when you rout each set of dadoes. The straightedge must be square to the edge of each side.

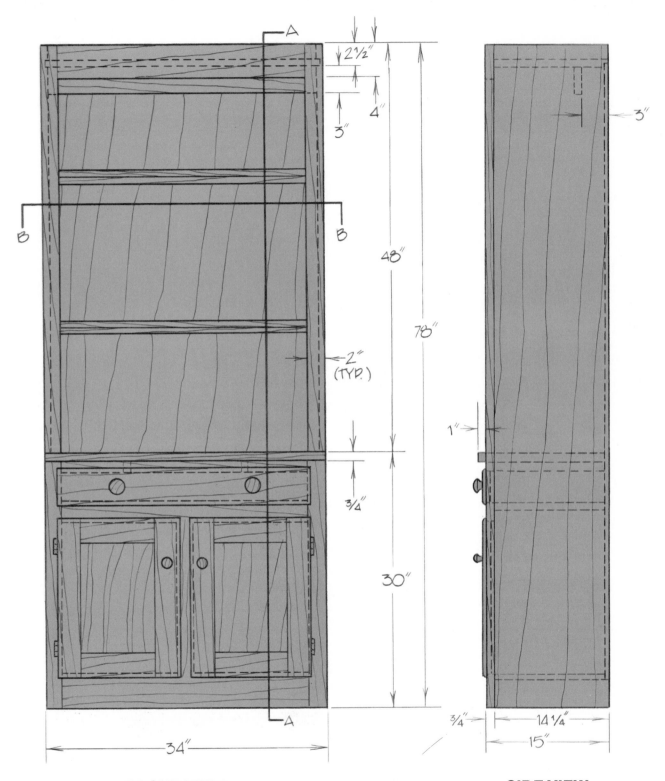

FRONT VIEW

SIDE VIEW

4 Drill the holes in the sides, back, and top.

Drill sets of stopped holes, ¼″ in diameter and ⅜″ deep, in both sides. These holes are shown in the *Side Layout*. When the wall unit is complete, the holes will hold pin-style shelving supports. These, in turn, will support the adjustable shelves in both the upper and lower sections of the case.

Cut ventilation holes through the top and the back, where shown in the *Top Layout* and *Back Layout*. These ventilation holes allow the heat from the cabinet lights to escape, preventing it from scorching the wood or causing it to warp. You also need these holes to run the electrical wires from the lamps through the top of the cabinet.

TRY THIS! To space the stopped holes in the sides evenly, make this simple jig and clamp it to your drill press fence. Use the jig as a stop to position the holes the same distance from each other. To use the jig, drill the first hole and put a peg in it. Slide the stock toward the stop until the peg hits it. Drill the next hole, move the peg from the first hole to the one you just drilled, and slide the stock again. Continue until you have drilled all the holes.

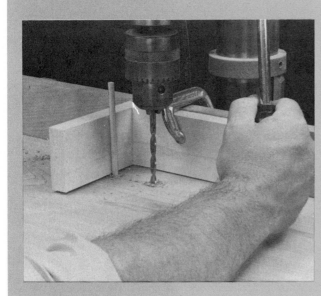

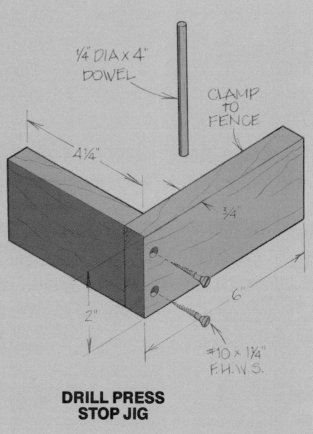

DRILL PRESS STOP JIG

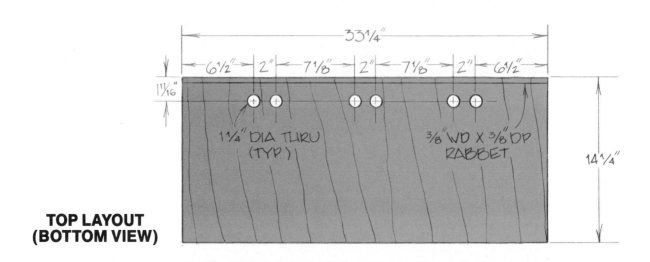

**TOP LAYOUT
(BOTTOM VIEW)**

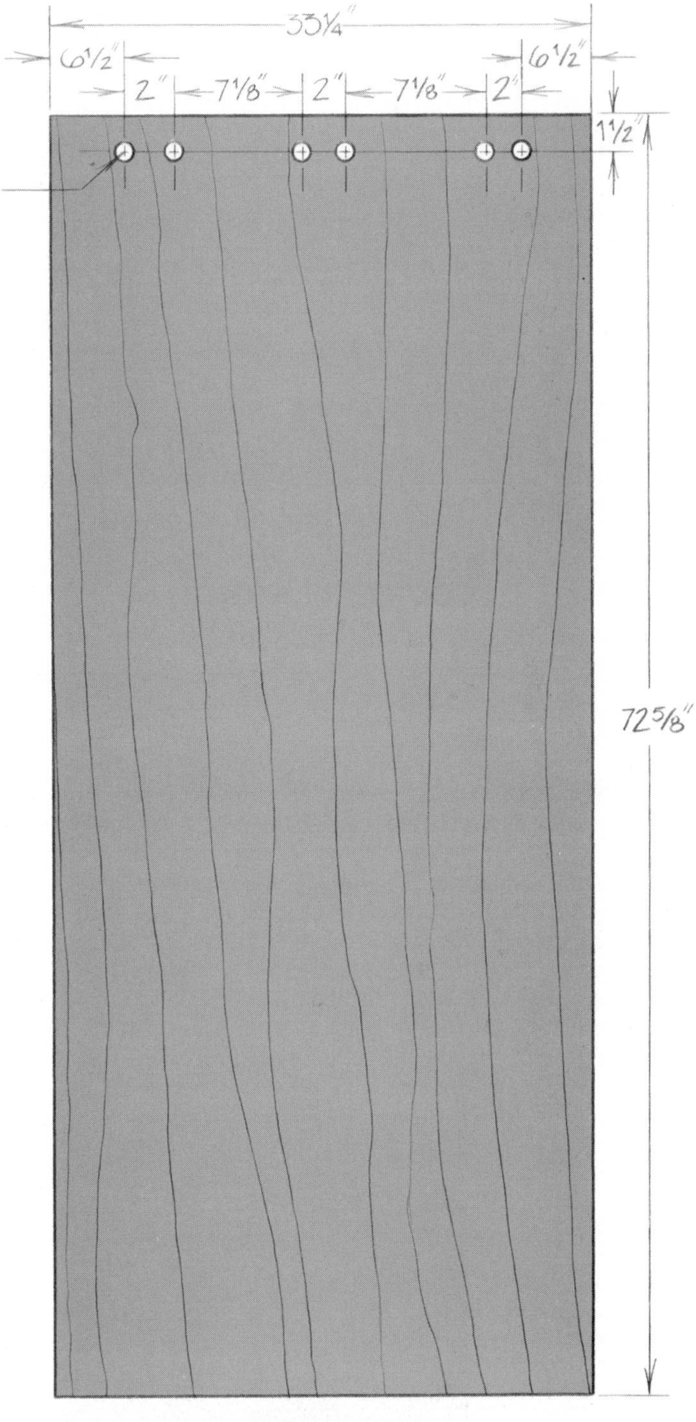

SIDE LAYOUT

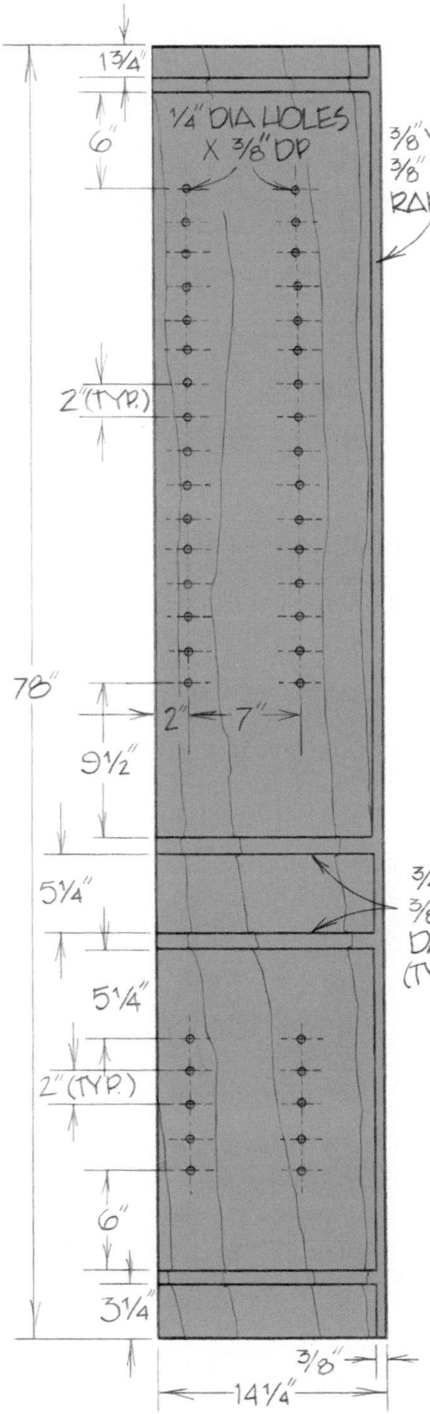

13/4"

6"

1/4" DIA HOLES
X 3/8" DP

3/8" WD X
3/8" DP
RABBET

2" (TYP.)

78"

2" — 7"

9½"

5¼"

3/4" WD X
3/8" DP
DADOES
(TYP.)

5¼"

2" (TYP.)

6"

3¼"

3/8"

14¼"

BACK LAYOUT

33¼"

6½"

2"

7⅛"

2"

7⅛"

2"

6½"

1½"

1¼" DIA
(TYP.)
THRU

72⅝"

5

Cut the shape of the counter. The counter — the middle fixed shelf in the case — must be notched to fit correctly. Cut the notches, as shown in the *Counter Layout,* with a band saw or a hand saw.

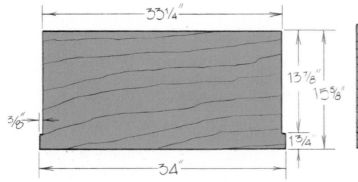

COUNTER LAYOUT

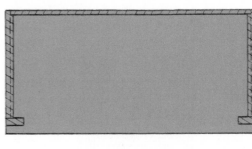

SECTION B

6

Build the web frame. The drawer is supported by a web frame inside the case. Assemble this frame with tongue-and-groove joinery. With a dado cutter or a router, make ¼″-wide, ⅜″-deep grooves in all the *inside* edges of the web-frame rails and stiles. (See Figure 2.) Cut grooves in both edges of the middle stile. Then cut ¼″-wide, ⅜″-long tongues on the ends of the stiles, using the same tool. (See Figure 3.)

Glue the rails and stiles together with the dust shields in place. *Do not* glue the dust shields in the grooves; let them float so that the assembly can expand and contract with changes in humidity.

When you clamp the rails and stiles of the web frame together, check that the assembly is square. The completed frame must be square if the drawer is to slide easily in and out of the case. After the glue dries on the rails and stiles, round the front edge of the drawer guide, as shown on the *Web-Frame Layout.* Attach the drawer guide to the *top* surface of the frame, centered on the middle stile.

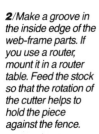

2/Make a groove in the inside edge of the web-frame parts. If you use a router, mount it in a router table. Feed the stock so that the rotation of the cutter helps to hold the piece against the fence.

3/Cut the tongues on the ends of the web-frame stiles with the aid of a miter gauge. Clamp a stop block to the fence to gauge the length of the tongue. This setup helps to prevent kickback.

7

Make the face frames. Join the members of the top and bottom face frames with dowels. Use a doweling jig to guide your drill when making the stopped dowel holes in the frame members. Glue the parts together, checking that the frames are square as you clamp them together.

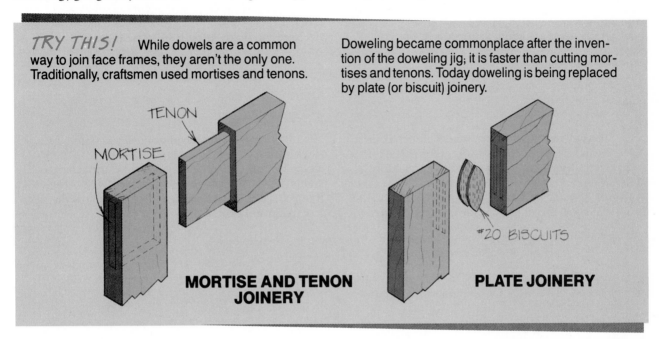

TRY THIS! While dowels are a common way to join face frames, they aren't the only one. Traditionally, craftsmen used mortises and tenons.

Doweling became commonplace after the invention of the doweling jig; it is faster than cutting mortises and tenons. Today doweling is being replaced by plate (or biscuit) joinery.

TENON

MORTISE

MORTISE AND TENON JOINERY

#20 BISCUITS

PLATE JOINERY

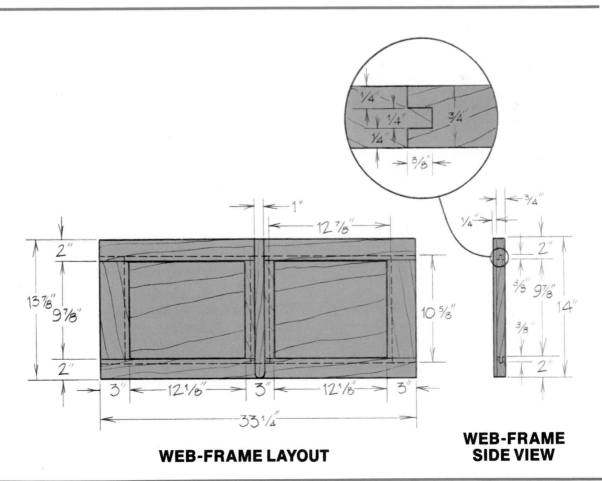

WEB-FRAME LAYOUT

WEB-FRAME SIDE VIEW

8

Finish sand the parts of the case. To ready the case parts for assembly, finish sand them — side, top, counter, shelves, bottom, back, light baffle, and face frames. You really don't need to finish sand the web frame, just smooth the parts. As you sand, be careful not to round over any edges or corners involved in the joints.

Note: It's best to completely assemble the case *before* you make the doors and drawer. That way, you can fit the doors and drawer to the case. If you have cut and assembled the case parts accurately, they won't need much fitting — just a little work with a hand plane or a file here and there. But it is still wise to wait.

9

Assemble the case. Assemble the case without glue to check the fit of the parts. Use band clamps to hold the parts together temporarily. When you're satisfied with the fit, reassemble the case with glue, screws, and brads. Assemble the parts in this order: First, join the sides, top, bottom, and counter.

Next, slide the web frame in place. If you've made the sides from plywood, you can glue the frame to them along the entire length of the dadoes. If the sides are solid wood, just apply glue to the first 1"-2" of the web frame (nearest the front edge). This will allow the sides to expand and contract.

TRY THIS! To reinforce the dado joints that join the sides to the top, bottom, counter, and web frame, drive #10 x 1¼" flathead wood screws from *inside* the case, so that they won't show on the outside. Angle the fasteners as if you were toe-nailing the parts together, but with screws instead

of nails. Drive the screws from inside and *underneath* the bottom, counter, and web frame, and inside and *above* the top. One more consideration: If the sides are made of solid wood, screws should be driven through the web frame *only* near the front edge — where it's glued to the sides.

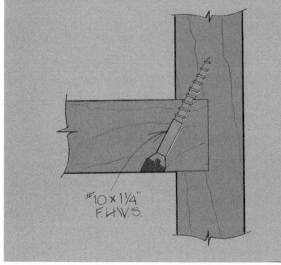

#10 x 1¼"
F.H.W.S.

As you clamp up this assembly, make sure that it is square. To help keep it square while the glue cures, tack the back in place with a few brads. *Do not* drive the brads home; leave the heads protruding so that you can easily remove them.

After the glue cures, remove the clamps and attach the face frames with glue. You can reinforce the frame-to-case joints with hidden splines or biscuits, but it isn't necessary. The parts all meet long grain to long grain, the grain directions are parallel, and there are no end grain or opposing grain joints, so a glue joint should be adequate.

After the glue has cured, remove the back and install the light baffle. Make screw pockets in the ends of the baffle on the *back* face. Glue the edge of the baffle to the top and hold it in place with screws. Secure the ends of the baffle by driving screws through the screw pockets and into the sides, as shown in the *Light Baffle-to-Side Joinery Detail.* Install the cabinet lights behind the baffle, screwing them to the top. Insert the cords through the ventilation holes in the top, then reinstall the back, fastening it with brads but no glue. You want to be able to remove the back easily just in case someday you may need to repair or replace the cabinet-light fixtures.

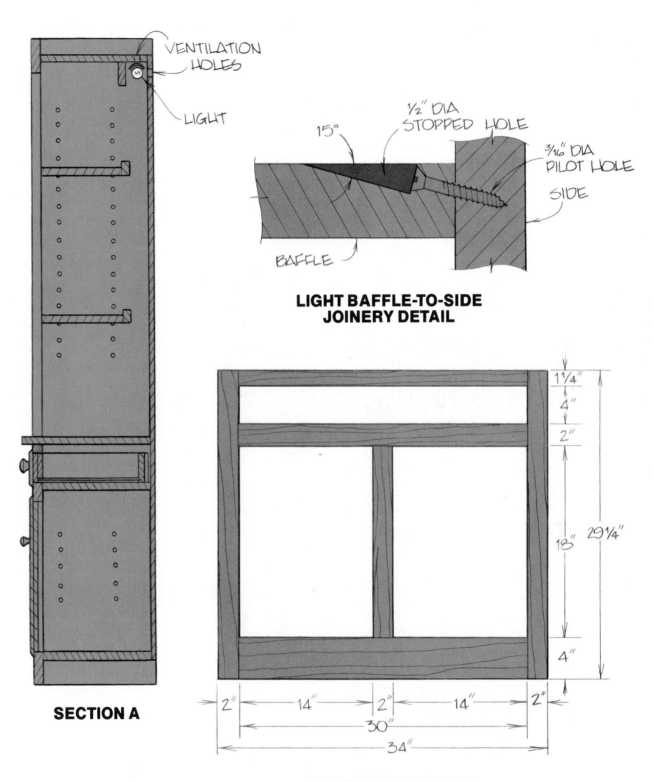

VENTILATION HOLES

LIGHT

15°

½" DIA. STOPPED HOLE

³⁄₁₆" DIA PILOT HOLE

SIDE

BAFFLE

LIGHT BAFFLE-TO-SIDE JOINERY DETAIL

SECTION A

1¼"

4"

2"

18"

29¼"

4"

2"

14"

2"

14"

2"

30"

34"

LOWER FACE FRAME FRONT VIEW

10

Make the drawer. Cut the joinery in the drawer parts. The front is joined to the sides with ⅜"-long half-blind dovetails, and the back with ¾"-wide, ⅜"-deep dadoes. The drawer bottom floats in ¼"-wide, ⅜"-deep grooves. You can make all of these joints with a router if you have a jig to cut the dovetails.

You can also use the router to round over the edges of the drawer face. Use a band saw or a hand saw to cut the notch in the bottom edge of the back, as shown in the *Drawer Back Layout*. This notch fits over the drawer guide and keeps the drawer properly positioned as it slides in and out of the case.

Finish sand the drawer face. Dry assemble the drawer to check the fit of the parts. Also check the fit of the drawer in the case. If both fits are good, reassemble the parts — including the face — with glue. Do not glue the bottom in the grooves; just let it float. Be sure the drawer is square when you clamp it together; otherwise, it may not work properly. After the glue cures, install the pulls and fit the drawer in the case.

TRY THIS! Rub the bottom edges of the assembled drawer with paraffin to help it slide smoothly in and out of the case.

11

Make the doors. Using a tenon-cutting jig and your table saw, cut tenons on the ends of the door stiles, and open mortises in the ends of the door stiles. (See Figure 4.) Assemble the door frames with glue and, once again, check that the assemblies are square as you clamp them together.

After the glue cures, rout ⅜"-wide, ⅜"-deep rabbets all around the inside of the frames to accept the door panels, and around the outside as well, to make the door lips. Square the corners of the *inside* rabbets with a chisel. Round over the front of the *outside* edges with a router to match the drawer face.

Finish sand the door frames and the door panels. Mount the panels in the frames, securing them with

4/Use a tenon-cutting jig to cut both parts of the bridle joints. The jig that you see here is store-bought, but you can easily make your own from scraps of wood.

small metal turn buttons, or "turn dogs," as they are sometimes called. Do not glue the panels in place; just let them float in the rabbets.

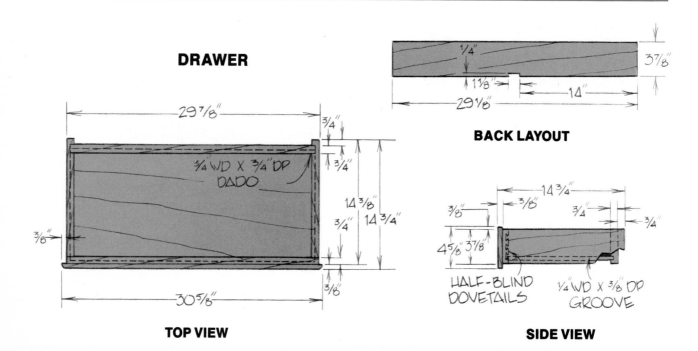

DRAWER

BACK LAYOUT

TOP VIEW

SIDE VIEW

12

Mount the doors in the case. Check the fit of the lipped doors in the case. The fit should not be tight — there should be a 1/16″ gap between the edge of the rabbets and the openings in the face frame. But the lips should completely cover the openings. If the door is too tight, use a bullnose plane or a *very* sharp chisel to pare away the edge of the rabbets.

When the doors fit to your satisfaction, mount them to the case with semi-concealed offset hinges. Depending on the make of these hinges, you may have to mortise them into the back of the doors. Install the pulls and catches, too. Depending on the type of catches you use, you may have to attach a mounting block to the back of the middle stile to hold them.

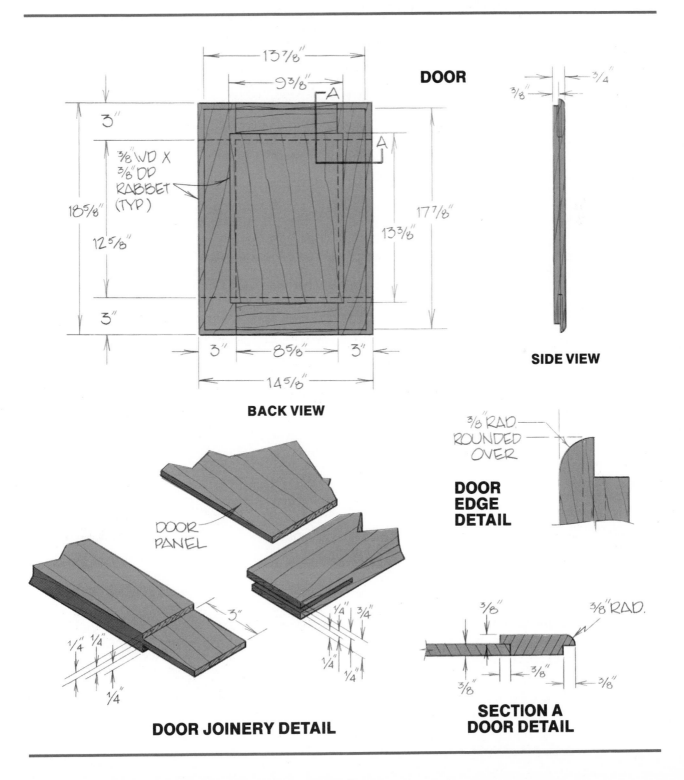

DOOR

SIDE VIEW

13 7/8″
9 3/8″
3″
3/8″ WD X
3/8″ DP
RABBET
(TYP)
18 5/8″
12 5/8″
17 7/8″
13 3/8″
3″
3″　8 5/8″　3″
14 5/8″

BACK VIEW

3/4
3/8

3/8″ RAD.
ROUNDED
OVER

DOOR EDGE DETAIL

DOOR
PANEL

3″
1/4″ 1/4″
1/4
1/4″ 3/4″
1/4″ 1/4″

DOOR JOINERY DETAIL

3/8″
3/8″
3/8″
3/8″ RAD.
3/8″

**SECTION A
DOOR DETAIL**

13 Make the top adjustable shelves.

Check the fit of the shelves in the case. If you're satisfied that they fit properly, finish sand the shelves and the backstops. Then glue the backstops to the top adjustable shelves. Place shelving supports in the holes in the sides where you want to hang the shelf — four supports to each shelf. Then lay the adjustable shelves in place.

The back edges of the top shelves should be just under two inches from the back. This will allow the light to flood the back of the case, backlighting all the shelves.

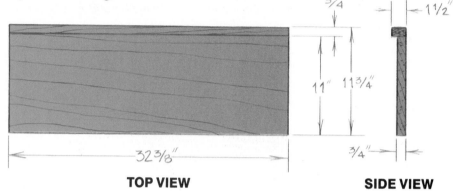

TOP ADJUSTABLE SHELF

3/4"   1 1/2"

11"   11 3/4"

3/4"

32 3/8"

TOP VIEW   **SIDE VIEW**

---

14 Wire the lights to a single switch.

Cabinet lights usually come with individual switches. What's more, the switches will be hidden behind the light baffle. Feeling around for the switch among the things that you have stored on the top shelf could easily be a hassle.

To avoid this, wire all three lights to a single switch, as shown in the *Cabinet Light Wiring Diagram*. Mount this switch in the top of the case, near the front so that you can easily reach it. (See Figure 5.) For now, *do not* solder the wires together, and don't staple the wires to the top. Use wire nuts so that you can test the circuit.

TO OUTLET

GROUND

HOT

CABINET LIGHTS

CABINET LIGHT WIRING DIAGRAM

SWITCH

5/Mount the switch in the top of the wall unit, near the front. Use a long-stem switch that will extend through the thickness of the wood. Make sure that the amperage of the switch is sufficient to handle all three lights. (A 100-watt light draws approximately 1 amp. Three 40-watt cabinet lights will draw less than 2 amps, so a standard 3-amp switch should handle the load safely.)

---

15 Finish the completed wall unit.

Remove the wires, switch, and lights from the wall unit to get it ready to finish. Remove the doors, drawer, adjustable shelves, and all the hardware, too.

Do any touch-up sanding necessary, then apply a finish to all the wood. Be sure to apply as many coats of finish to the inside of the case as you do to the outside. If the finish is uneven, one side of a board may absorb moisture faster than the other side, which eventually could cause the board to warp, distorting the case.

After the finish dries, reinstall the doors, drawers, shelves, hardware, and lighting. Solder the wires together permanently and wrap the connections in electrical tape or heat-shrinkable tubing. Staple the wires to the upper face of the top (where you can't see them).

Adjustable Shelving Hardware

If you're building a storage project with *adjustable* shelves — shelves that you can raise or lower at will — there are several types of hardware that you can choose from to support them. Here are the most common types:

Standards and brackets — Shelving standards are long strips of metal with *vertical* slots. The standards mount on the wall or the back of a cabinet. The vertical slots hold brackets, which, in turn, hold shelves. (See A on the chart.) The ends of the brackets have hooks that keep them from sliding out of the slots and usually some sort of a locking screw to keep them from working loose. To adjust the height of a shelf, remove the brackets from the slots where they're currently positioned and move them to another slot. Standards and brackets are very strong, but they look like raw hardware — there's a lot of metal showing.

Pilasters and clips — Pilasters look a great deal like standards, but they have *horizontal* slots. They mount on the sides of a cabinet. The horizontal slots hold clips that support the shelves at the ends. (See B.) The clips "snap" into the slots. To adjust the height of a shelf, move the four clips supporting it to the proper slots

— much the same as you do to adjust the brackets. Using pilasters and clips, you don't see as much metal as you do with standards and brackets, but the pilasters still show.

L-shaped pin supports — Pin shelving supports come in a variety of shapes and materials. The most common is an L-shape with a ¼″-diameter pin attached to the upright of the "L." (See C.) There are also "spoon-shaped" pin supports and "locking" pin supports. The spoon-shaped support flattens out from the pin, and the locking support grips both the upper and lower surface of the shelf. (See D and E.) In use, the pin fits in a hole in the side of the cabinet, and the shelf rests on its extension. To adjust the shelf, just move the four pin supports to another set of holes. The advantage of pin supports is that they are extremely easy to install, and you hardly see the hardware.

Wire supports — Wire supports (sometimes called magic wire or Swedish-style supports) are lengths of steel rod that are bent to hold the shelves. The ends of the wire supports fit into holes in the sides of the cabinet, and the wire itself fits into a slot in the end of the shelf. (See F.) To adjust the height of a shelf, move the wire supports to another set of holes. Using wire supports, you don't see any hardware at all.

***Common Shelving Support Hardware**/These shelving supports are readily available at most hardware and building supply stores, as well as from mail-order woodworking suppliers. They are: (A) standards and brackets, (B) pilasters and clips, (C) L-shaped pin supports, (D) spoon-shaped pin supports, (E) locking pin supports, and (F) wire supports.*

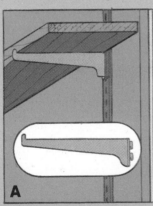

Standards and brackets

Pilasters and clips

L-shaped pin supports

Spoon-shaped pin supports

Locking pin supports

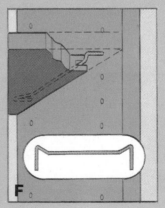

Wire supports

Adjustable Bookcase

Among the simplest — and most versatile — storage projects you can build is an adjustable bookcase. As you can see in the exploded view, it's really nothing more than a box with a face frame. Because of this simplicity, it can be easily changed to accommodate anything from a set of encyclopedias to a video library to a collection of old tools — almost anything you want to display. You can change the depth, width, or height without changing the construction at all.

Because the shelves are not fixed in the bookcase, the project remains adaptable, even after you've completed it. As your needs change and you acquire different items to store on the shelves, you can easily rearrange the level of these shelves. Furthermore, you have many choices as to how you will support the shelves. There are several hardware systems you can buy or wooden systems you can build to install adjustable shelves in a case. Some of these systems will support heavier loads; others simply change the appearance of the bookcase. We'll discuss many of these options to help you design and build the bookcase that best suits your needs and your tastes. ✸

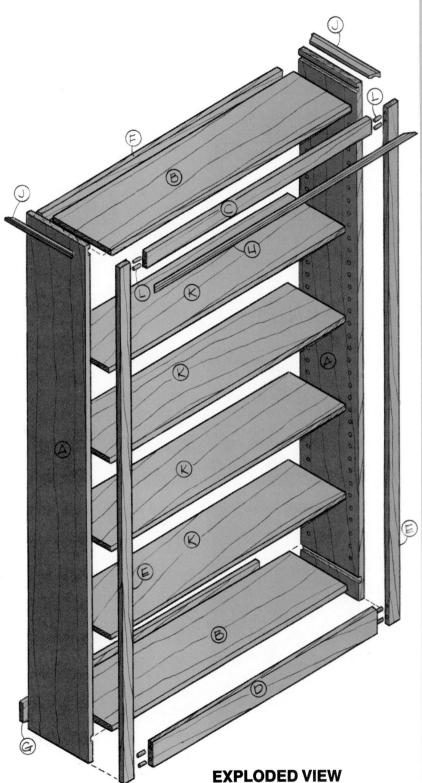

EXPLODED VIEW

Materials List

FINISHED DIMENSIONS

PARTS

A.	Sides (2)	¾" x 11¼" x 83"
B.	Top/bottom (2)	¾" x 11¼" x 46¼"
C.	Face frame top rail	¾" x 2¾" x 43"
D.	Face frame bottom rail	¾" x 4" x 43"
E.	Face frame stiles (2)	¾" x 2" x 83"
F.	Top cleat	¾" x 2" x 45½"
G.	Bottom cleat	¾" x 3¼" x 45½"
H.	Front cove molding	¾" x 2⅝" x 50¾"
J.	Side cove moldings (2)	¾" x 2⅝" x 13⅞"
K.	Adjustable shelves (4-6)	¾" x 11⅛" x 45⅜"*
L.	Dowels (8)	⅜" dia. x 2"

This dimension may change slightly, depending on the hardware you use to support the shelves.

HARDWARE

1¼" x #8 Flathead wood screws (24-36)
Shelving supports (16-24)

1

Determine the style of bookcase you want to build. The bookcase shown here is built in a contemporary style. However, you can change the style to suit your own tastes by simply adding or elim-

inating moldings and other shaped parts. We show three suggested styles in the working drawings: *Traditional, Contemporary,* and *Country.* Use one of these, or create your own.

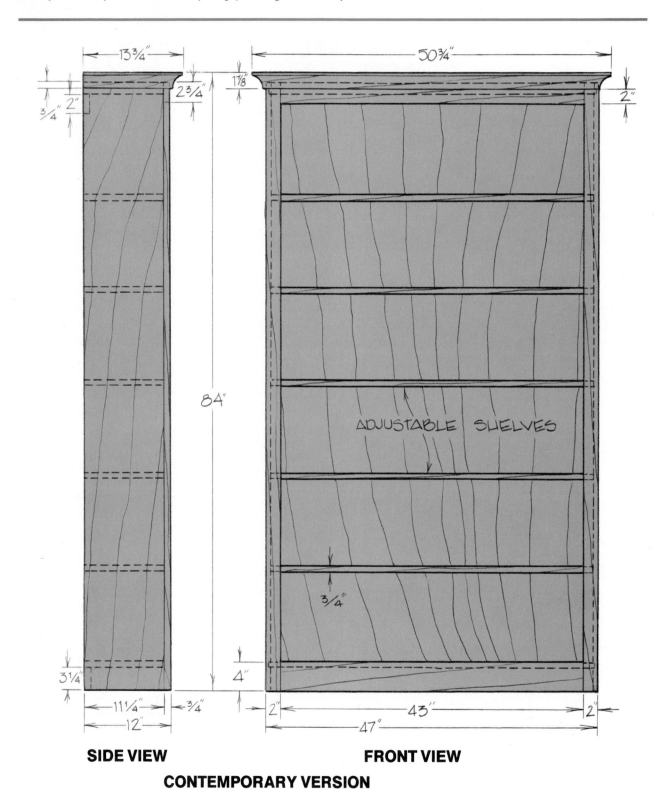

SIDE VIEW   **FRONT VIEW**

CONTEMPORARY VERSION

2 Determine the dimensions of the bookcase you want to build.

Once you have settled on a style, decide the size of the bookcase. There are three things to take into consideration:

The space you have available for the bookcase — The most important consideration is how much space you have in your home for a bookcase. Is this space horizontal or vertical? Can you build the shelves floor-to-ceiling, as we have done here, or should they be shorter? How long can you make the shelves?

Note: Because of the manner in which the top molding is attached to the case, the top of the bookcase should be above your line of sight. If you want to make a shorter bookcase, whose top is below your line of sight, attach the top shelf and the molding differently, as shown in the *Short Bookcase Top Detail*.

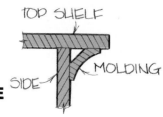

SHORT BOOKCASE TOP DETAIL

What you have to store on the shelves — What sorts of items do you want to put on the shelves? How many books, trophies, and knickknacks do you want to display? How big are they?

The distance between supports — How far apart can you place the supporting sides of the bookcase? If you're building from hardwood, the span should be no more than 48″. If you're making the shelves from softwood, no more than 36″.

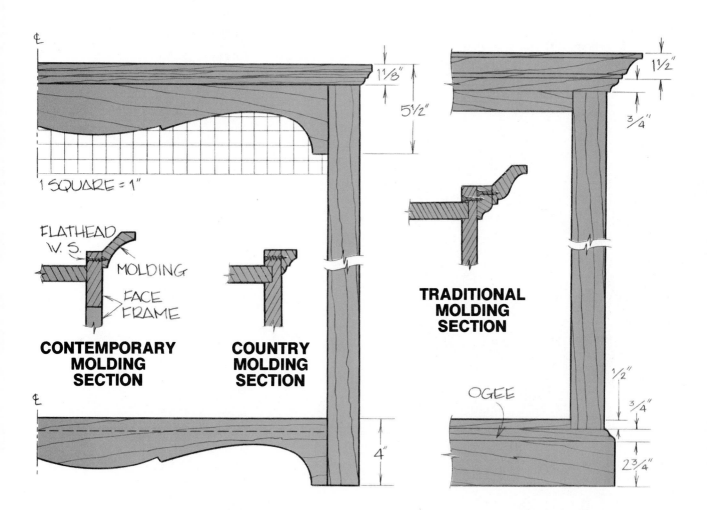

CONTEMPORARY MOLDING SECTION

COUNTRY MOLDING SECTION

TRADITIONAL MOLDING SECTION

FRONT VIEW COUNTRY VERSION

FRONT VIEW TRADITIONAL VERSION

3

Draw up a plan. Once you have decided on the style and the size of your bookcase, make a plan. It doesn't have to be anything fancy. A sketch will do. Then revise the Materials List.

4

Cut all parts to size. Cut the parts to the sizes you have calculated in your revised Materials List. Cut the stock for the moldings 1″-2″ longer than needed, to give you room to cut the miters.

5

Cut the joinery in the sides. The bottom and top are attached to the sides by ¾″-wide, ⅜″-deep dadoes. Cut these joints with a dado cutter or a router.

The adjustable shelves in this bookcase are supported by metal or plastic pins, called "shelving supports." These supports fit in holes in the sides. Mark the locations of these holes on the *inside* face of the sides, as shown in the *Side Layout.* Then drill ¼″-diameter, ⅜″-deep stopped holes wherever you've put a mark.

TRY THIS! Drilling all these holes can be tedious. To help this chore go faster, use a simple jig to help space the holes. Drill a hole and put a peg in it. Slide the board to the right until the peg hits the stop, then drill another hole. Remove the peg from the first hole, put it into the hole you just drilled, and repeat.

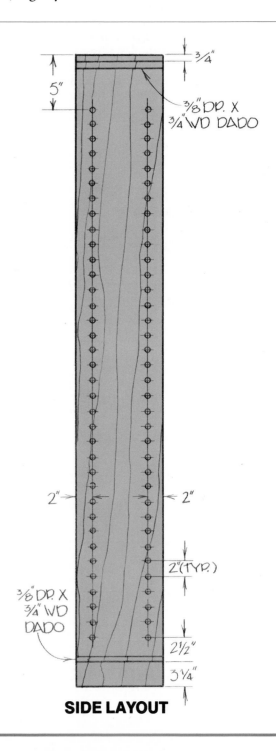

¾″

5″

⅜″ DP. X ¾″ WD DADO

2″   2″

2″ (TYP.)

⅜″ DP. X ¾″ WD DADO

2½″

3¼″

SIDE LAYOUT

6

Shape the moldings and any other parts that require it. Cut the shapes of the moldings, stiles, and rails to match the style that you have selected. Most of the moldings can be made with a shaper or a router, and the rails and stiles with a band saw or sabre saw. But the cove moldings on the "contemporary" bookcase require some fancy work with a table saw and a jointer.

Clamp a board to the worktable of your table saw to guide the molding stock over the blade, 23° off parallel to the blade. Lower the saw blade until it's cutting no more than 1⁄8″-1⁄4″ deep. Run the molding stock over the saw blade several times, cutting no more than 1⁄8″ deeper with each pass. Continue until the cove is 1⁄2″ deep. (See Figure 1.)

Tilt the fence of your jointer to 45°, so that it leans in toward the knives. Adjust the depth of cut to 5⁄32″. Bevel

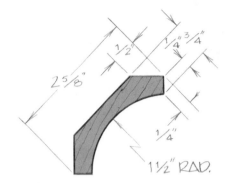

COVE MOLDING DETAIL

all four corners of the stock, making *two* passes over the knives to cut the *front* corners, and *four* passes to cut the *back* corners. (See Figure 2.)

Scrape and sand the concave surface of the moldings to remove the saw marks.

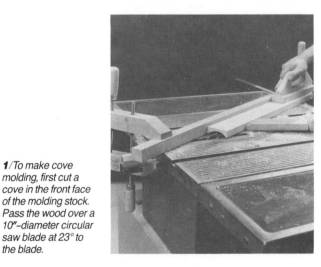

1/To make cove molding, first cut a cove in the front face of the molding stock. Pass the wood over a 10″-diameter circular saw blade at 23° to the blade.

2/Finish the molding by beveling the corners at 45° on a jointer.

7

Assemble the face frame. Join the face frame rails and stiles with dowels. Use a doweling jig to help position and drill the dowel holes; then assemble the parts with glue. As you clamp up the frame, check that it's square. Incidentally, you can also use a "biscuit machine" and biscuits to join the parts, if you have this tool.

8

Finish sand all the parts. Finish sand the face frame assembly and all the unassembled parts. Be careful not to round over those edges where boards will be joined together.

9

Assemble the bookcase. Join the sides, top, bottom, and cleats with glue and screws. Clamp up the case assembly and make sure it's square. Drill pilot holes for the screws, counterboring and countersinking them. Drive the screws, then cover the heads with wooden plugs so they won't show. When the glue dries, join the face frame to the case with glue and screws. Finally, attach the moldings. Once again, use glue and screws, but drive the screws from the *inside* of the case so that you won't have to cover them. (See Figure 3.)

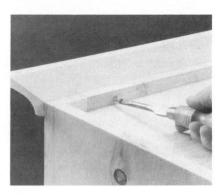

3/Attach the moldings to the case by driving the screws through the case from the inside, then into the moldings. This way, the screws won't show.

10

Finish the bookcase. Cut the wooden plugs flush with the surface of the stock. Finish sand the joints and any other parts that may still need it. Then apply a finish to the completed case.

Step-by-Step: Making Moldings

You can easily make your own moldings with a router or a shaper. Simply cut a shape in the edge or the surface of a board.

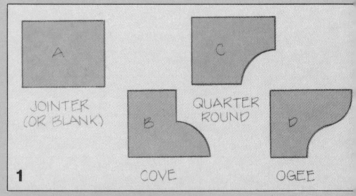

Router bits and shaper cutters come in a variety of simple shapes. Here are six shapes most commonly used to make moldings: (A) Jointer, (B) Cove, (C) Quarter-round, (D) Ogee, (E) Vee, and (F) Bead.

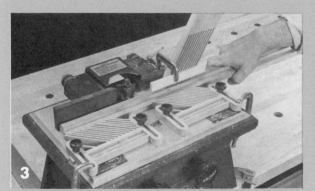

Precision is important when you make moldings with multiple passes. If you're using a router, be sure to use a guide fence. If you're using a shaper, use featherboards to help hold the stock firmly against the fence and the worktable. Also, make a great deal more molding than you think you'll need. This will give you extra stock to use as "test pieces" as you set up the router or the shaper for each successive pass.

If you need to make thin or narrow moldings, never try to shape or rout small pieces of stock. Small pieces will splinter or come apart as you are cutting them, throwing slivers of wood at you. Instead, shape the edge of a wide board…

11 **Install the shelves.** After the finish dries, clean out the shelving support holes in the sides with a ¼″-diameter drill bit. This will remove any finish that may have beaded up inside the holes. Use a stop on the drill, so that you don't accidentally drill through the sides. Insert shelving supports in the holes wherever you want them, and lay the shelves in place.

12 **Attach the bookcase to the wall, if necessary.** Tall bookcases, such as the one shown here, present a danger that must be avoided: They may tip over — particularly if the floor isn't perfectly level. To prevent this, drill holes in the top cleats and attach the bookcase to the wall with wall anchors.

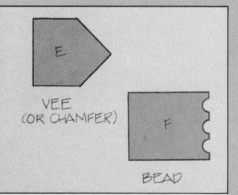

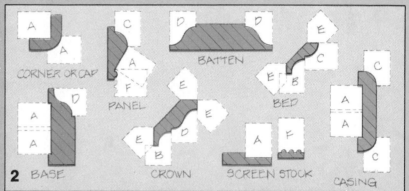

Many moldings are formed with a combination of shapes. These must be cut in several passes, sometimes using a different bit or cutter for each pass. These drawings show how to combine the simple shapes to make eight common moldings.

5

...then rip the molding from the edge. To protect your fingers and help keep the molding from "kicking back" once it's cut, push the molding past the blade with a push stick.

6

If you must rip molding from a short board (less than 18″ long) set up your table saw so that the molding is cut to the outside of the blade, not between the blade and the fence. If you rip a short molding between the blade and the fence, it will kick back with tremendous force.

Bracket Shelves

One of the most versatile and economical shelving projects you can build are "bracket" shelves.

These shelves mount to an unused wall, allowing you to use the entire wall — or any portion of it — for storage. You can install the shelves floor to ceiling, if you wish, or just mount a few up high to take advantage of the wasted space above furniture and base cabinets. Since they don't have side supports or backs, they don't require as much lumber (or as much expense) as stand-alone shelving units.

Bracket shelves, as shown here, are also a good deal sturdier than many other shelving units. The shelves and the aprons form an L-beam, strengthening the span between brackets. And since the project is attached directly to the frame of your house, it can support enormous loads.

You can change the look of the shelves to blend with almost any decor, simply by changing the shape of the aprons and brackets. The shelves you see here are traditional, but we also show patterns for country and contemporary brackets and aprons.

Materials List

FINISHED DIMENSIONS

PARTS

A. Shelf   ¾" x 8" x (variable)

B. Brackets
(variable)   1½" x 5½" x 7¼"

C. Aprons
(variable)   ¾" x 2¾" x (variable)

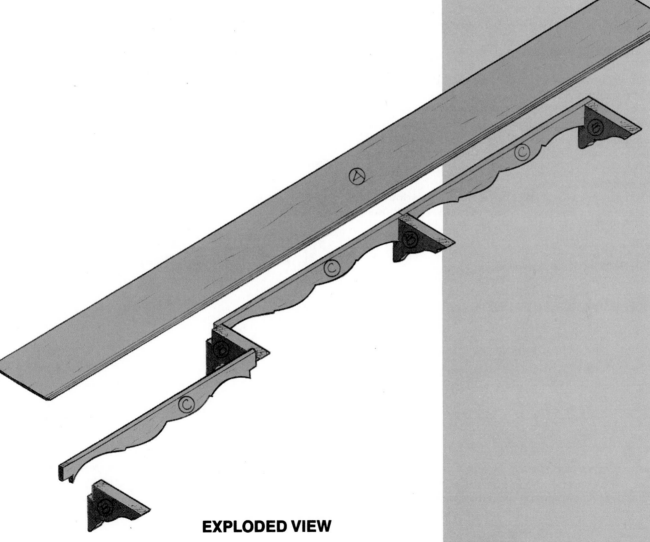

EXPLODED VIEW

HARDWARE

#10 x 1½" Flathead wood screws
(variable)
#12 x 3" Flathead wood screws
(variable)

1 ***Decide how and where you want to attach the shelves to your wall.*** Determine the composition of the wall where you intend to hang these shelves. Is it a frame wall with drywall or plaster? Concrete block or masonry? This will help you determine *how* you're going to hang the completed shelves. If it's a frame wall, you can use ordinary wood screws or hollow wall anchors. If the wall is made from concrete block or masonry, you'll have to use expansion shields. (See Figures 1, 2, and 3.)

If you're going to hang the shelf on a frame wall, you also need to find the locations of the studs. The studs not only establish where you're going to attach the shelf to the wall, they help determine where you'll place the brackets. There are two basic techniques for locating studs. The least messy is to use some sort of a "stud finder." The most accurate is the "bang-and-poke" method.

Measure where you're going the put the shelf. One to two inches *below* the level of the shelf, begin to tap lightly on the wall with a hammer. The spaces in between the studs will sound hollow; the studs themselves will sound solid. When you think you've located a stud, drive an 8d finishing nail into the wall. If you meet with little resistance, you've missed the stud. Pull the nail out of the wall and try again an inch or so to the right or left. Eventually, you'll hit the stud.

You may put a lot of holes in the wall 'til all is done. The holes, however, will be completely covered by the apron when you hang the shelves. If you ever take the shelves down, you can easily fill in the small holes with spackling.

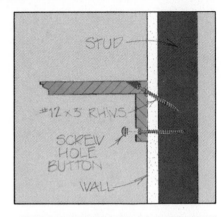

1/Use #14 x 3" roundhead wood screws to attach the shelf to the studs in a frame wall.

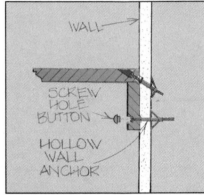
2/If the location of one or more of the studs is inconvenient, you may have to attach some part of the shelf to the hollow wall, using hollow wall anchors. Remember, these anchors will not support as much weight as wood screws or expansion shields.

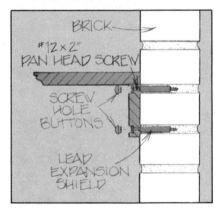
3/To attach the shelf to a concrete block or masonry wall, use expansion shields.

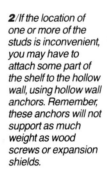

TRY THIS! No matter what method you use, the first stud is always the hardest to find. After you find one, you can be fairly certain that the next one is either 16" or 24" away — 16" if you have an older home, and 24" if your home was built in the last ten or fifteen years.

2 ***Plan your shelf.*** Decide how long to make the shelf and where you want to place the brackets. If you intend to mount the shelf on a frame wall, you want to position the individual brackets between studs. The longest span *between* the brackets should be 30".

3 ***Cut the parts to size.*** Cut the parts you need to make the shelves. Rip both the shelf and apron stock from 1 x 12 lumber, and cut the brackets from 2 x 6 lumber.

4 *Cut the shapes of the aprons and brackets.*

Enlarge the parts for the aprons and brackets. You will probably have to expand or contract the apron pattern, since the distance between brackets is variable. This is easily done by making one section on the *horizontal* scale equal to some measurement other than the 1″ shown on the *Apron Pattern*.

Note that the ends of the aprons are "tenons" that fit into 1½″-wide, ¾″-deep notches in the backs of the brackets. The apron tenons that fit into *end* brackets are 1½″ long. The tenons that fit into *middle* brackets are just ¾″ long, since these brackets are joined to two aprons — one on either side. (See Figure 4.)

Trace the patterns onto the stock. Then cut out the shapes with a band saw or sabre saw.

4/The ends of the aprons are "tenons" that fit into notches in the brackets. The end brackets accommodate one long tenon; the middle brackets, two short tenons.

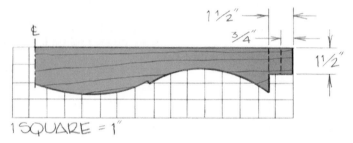

APRON PATTERN

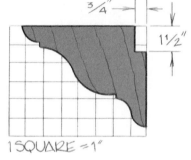

BRACKET PATTERN

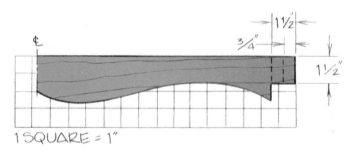

COUNTRY APRON PATTERN

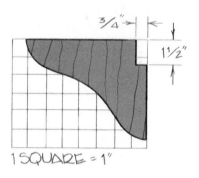

COUNTRY BRACKET PATTERN

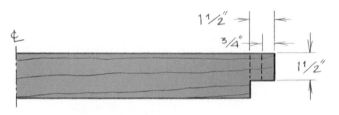

CONTEMPORARY APRON

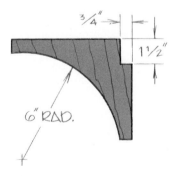

CONTEMPORARY BRACKET

5

Shape the edges of the shelves. As shown in the *Edge Details,* the shelves have an ogee-shaped edge. This creates an optical illusion that makes the shelves seem thinner and more delicate than they really are. Use a router to shape the edges. Shape the ends first, then the long front edge.

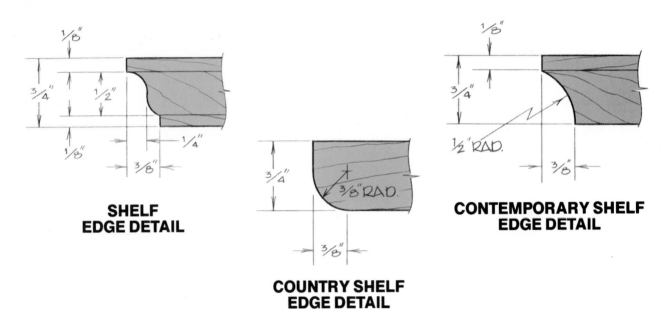

**SHELF
EDGE DETAIL**

**COUNTRY SHELF
EDGE DETAIL**

**CONTEMPORARY SHELF
EDGE DETAIL**

6

Finish sand all parts. Sand the shelves, aprons, and brackets to remove the millmarks and get the parts ready for finishing. Be careful not to round over any corners or edges that join other parts.

7

Assemble the shelves. Attach the aprons to the brackets with glue and flathead screws. Countersink the screws so that the heads are flush with the back surface of the aprons. Then attach the shelves to the brackets and aprons with glue and screws. Counterbore and countersink the screws, then cover the heads with wooden plugs.

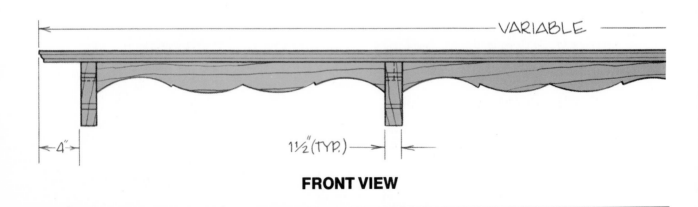

FRONT VIEW

8

Temporarily attach the shelves to the wall. With a helper, position the shelf on the wall. Drill ⅛″-diameter holes through the aprons and into the wall to mark where you want to put the fasteners. Take the shelf down and counterbore the aprons for screws or bolts. Don't make the counterbores any larger than ½″ in diameter, so that you can cover the heads of the fasteners with wooden screw-hole buttons. Install hollow wall anchors or expansion shields in the walls, if you are using them. Then hang the shelf on the wall to check that it's level.

TRY THIS! Professional carpenters often use "dead men" to help hang wall cabinets and shelves. These are just 2 x 4s, cut so that they're just a little longer than needed to prop the project up off the ground. Use the dead men to support the project at the proper height by angling the bottoms of the 2 x 4s away from the wall slightly. Level the project by angling the dead man that holds up one end a little more or a little less than the dead man holding up the other end.

9

Apply a finish to the shelves. Take the shelf down from the wall and finish sand any wooden parts that may still need it. Apply a stain or finish to the completed shelves. Stain or finish the wooden buttons to match.

10

Permanently attach the shelves to the wall. After the finish dries, hang the the shelves on the wall permanently. Cover the heads of the screws or bolts with the buttons. If you're putting the shelves up to stay, glue the buttons in place. If you think that you might take the shelves down for some reason, just press the buttons in place. That way, you can easily remove the buttons — and the shelves — should you ever want to.

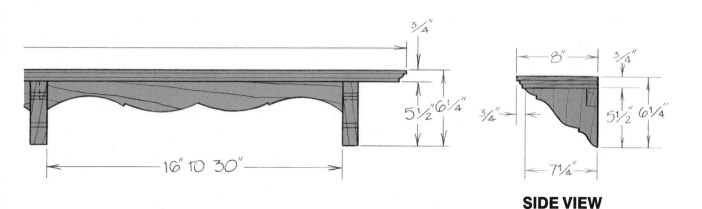

SIDE VIEW

Blanket Chest

Storage chests, like the one you see here, were among the first pieces of furniture ever built on this continent. The settlers used them for everything. They kept all their worldly possessions in them; they sat on them, slept on them, even hid behind them when the Indians attacked.

Today, these chests remain just as useful. You may no longer be in danger of wild Indians, but you probably have a good many more things to store than the settlers had. Chests will store a wide variety of items that fall into the "occasional use" category we mentioned in the

Introduction — linens, seasonal clothes, sports equipment, and so on. Because most chests do double duty as low tables, you don't want to put things in them that you use very often. If you do, you'll be constantly moving things off the top of the chest to get at the contents. But they're great for medium-to-long-term storage.

The chest shown here is more than just a storage unit. The sides are joined with through dovetails, and the lid is attached to the chest with wooden hinges. Touches like these are the hallmarks of good

craftsmanship and distinguish the hand-wrought from the store-bought. They also help to turn a simple storage unit into storage art.

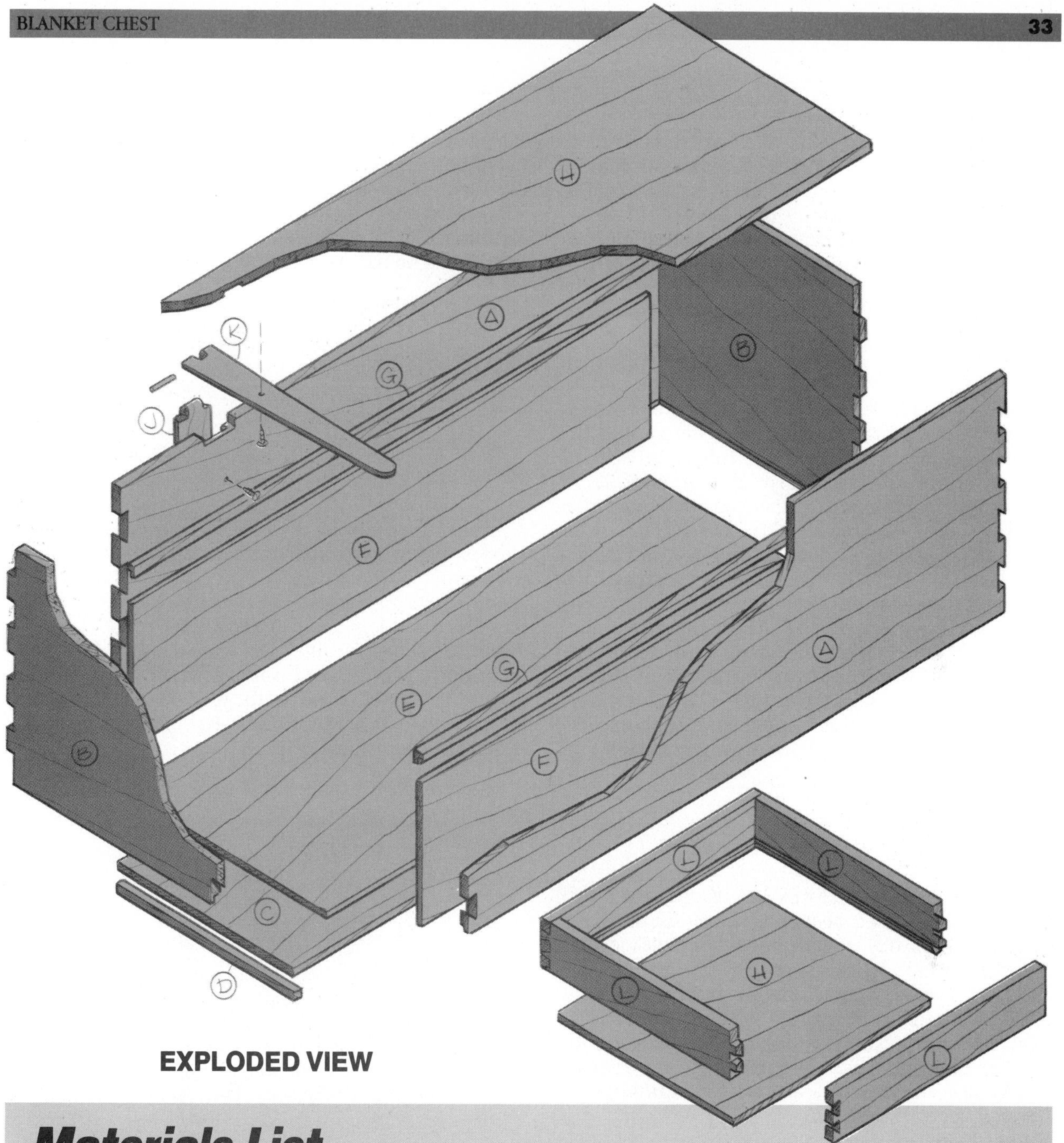

EXPLODED VIEW

Materials List

FINISHED DIMENSIONS

PARTS

A.	Sides (2)	¾″ x 19¼″ x 53″
B.	Ends (2)	¾″ x 19¼″ x 21½″
C.	Bottom	½″ x 20¾″ x 52¼″
D.	Feet (3)	¾″ x 1″ x 20¾″
E.	Bottom lining	⅜″ x 20″ x 51½″
F.	Side linings (2)	⅜″ x 12″ x 51½″
G.	Runners (2)	¾″ x 1″ x 51½″
H.	Lid	¾″ x 22″ x 54″
J.	Chest hinge leaves (2)	¾″ x 2¾″ x 17⅜″*
K.	Lid hinge leaves (2)	¾″ x 2¾″ x 20⅜″*
L.	Tray sides/ ends (4)	¾″ x 4½″ x 19⅞″
M.	Tray bottom	¼″ x 19″ x 19″

HARDWARE

4d Finishing nails (¼ lb.)
¾″ Brads (1 box)
#8 x 1¼″ Flathead wood screws (9)
#8 x ¾″ Flathead wood screws (4)*
3/16″ Hinge pins (2)*

These parts and hardware are optional.

1 **Cut the parts to size.** To make this chest, you'll need approximately 36 board feet of "four-quarter" stock, surfaced to ¾" thick, 16 square feet of ⅜" cedar "closet lining," and one 4' x 8' sheet of ½"-thick plywood. Use the solid stock to make the chest sides, ends, lid, tray sides, and other small parts; the cedar to line the chest; and the plywood for the chest bottom and the tray bottom. *Don't* use plywood for the sides or ends of this chest.

Note: The chest you see here is made from poplar, but there are dozens of other suitable cabinet-grade woods that you might choose. You may, in fact, choose two *contrasting* woods to make the chest, using one species for the ends and the other for the sides. This would help to show off the dovetail joinery. Here are some possible choices: walnut and cherry, walnut and butternut, cherry and maple, cherry and birch, red oak and ash, white oak and hickory, sassafras and poplar. *Caution:* Avoid mixing open- and close-grained woods. These don't expand and contract at the same rate.

Glue up the wide stock you'll need to make the sides, ends, and lid. When joining the boards for the sides and ends, make sure that the growth rings all curve in the same direction — toward the *outside*. The wood will tend to cup toward the inside, but this is easily controlled by the joinery. The dovetail joints at the corners keep the sides and ends flat. When gluing up stock for the lid, *alternate* the direction of the rings — one up, one down, etc. Use narrow boards, approximately 5"-6" wide. This way, if the wood does cup, the whole lid won't cup in one direction. The lid may get a little "wavy," but it will still lie fairly flat on the chest.

TRY THIS! If you can get it, purchase quarter-sawn or rift-sawn lumber for the lid. It's more expensive than plain-sawn, but this type of lumber is more stable and less prone to warping and cupping.

After you've glued up the wide stock, cut all the parts to the sizes shown in the Materials List. Note that the wooden hinges are difficult parts to make and fit, requiring a fair amount of hand work. Creating these hinges is rewarding, and they add a great deal to the aesthetic value of the chest. But if you'd rather not make them, don't. Instead, add a pair of decorative strap hinges to the "Hardware" section of the list. You can find these hinges with "gate hardware" in most building-supply centers and hardware stores.

2 **Cut the dovetails in the chest and tray parts.** As we mentioned before, the parts of the chest and the tray are joined with "through" dovetails — both the tails and the pins are visible, no matter where you stand to view the chest. How you make these dovetails is a highly individual matter. Most craftsmen make them either by hand or with the aid of a router and a template, although you can also use a band saw or a table saw. We've covered one possible method in *Making Through Dovetails with a Jig*.

When laying out your dovetails, note that the bottom corner of the bottom pin comes no closer to the bottom edge than ¾", as shown in the *Dovetail Detail.* Also note that the tails are cut in the sides, and the pins are cut in the ends. *This is important!* If you switch the location of the pins and tails, or cut the pins too close to the bottom edge, the joinery that holds the chest bottom or the tray bottom may show. This will spoil the appearance of the dovetails.

The angle of the dovetails in the *Dovetail Detail* is 10°. The angle is not an absolute, however. You may cut the dovetails at any angle you wish. Most handmade dovetails are angled somewhere between 7° and 12°.

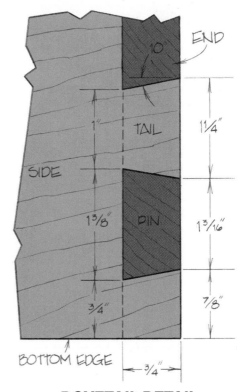

DOVETAIL DETAIL
SIDE VIEW

3 Cut the rabbets, grooves, and notches in the chest and tray parts.

With a router or a dado cutter, make ½"-wide, ⅜"-deep rabbets in the bottom edge of the sides and ends, as shown in the *Bottom Joinery Detail*. The rabbets in the sides (the parts with the tails) should be "double-blind" — they should not be cut through to either end of the stock. Instead, stop these rabbets ⅜" shy of the ends, and square the round "blind" corners with a chisel. (See Figure 1.) If you cut these rabbets through, you'll be able to see them when you assemble the chest.

Cut ½"-wide, ⅜"-deep grooves in the tray sides and ends, as shown in the *Tray Joinery Detail*. Like the rabbets in the chest parts, the grooves in the tray sides — the parts with the *tails* — should be stopped ⅜" shy of the ends. Square off the blind ends of the grooves with a

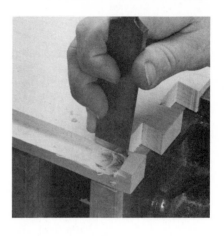

1/The rabbets and the grooves in the sides of the chest and the tray are "double-blind" — stopped at both ends so that they won't show when the project is assembled. Square the ends of these joints with a chisel.

chisel. Finally, cut two 2¾"-wide, ⅜"-deep notches in the top edge of the back side, where shown in the *Back Side View*, to accept the wooden hinges.

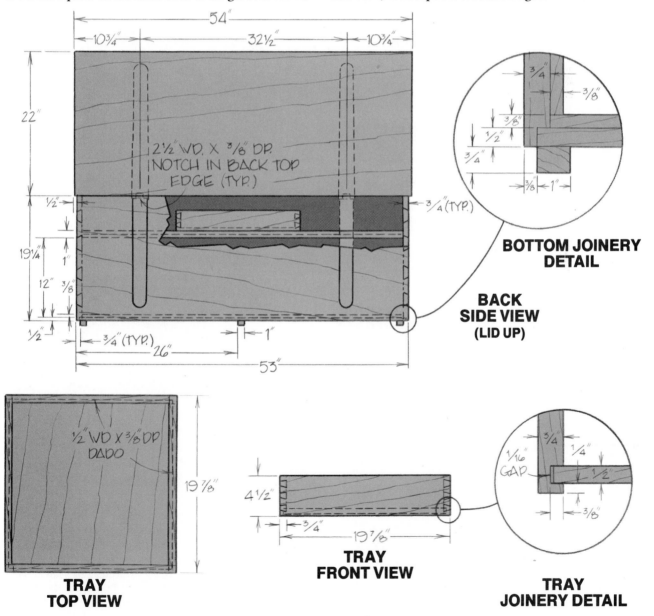

4 **Make and fit the knuckles at the ends of the hinge leaves.** While the hinge leaf stock is still square, drill ³⁄₁₆″-diameter holes for the hinge pin, where shown in the *Chest Hinge Leaf Detail* and the *Lid Hinge Leaf Detail*. On a band saw, cut the knuckles in each of the leaves. To ensure accuracy, cut a little wide of the layout line, then sand down to the line. With a chisel and a fine rasp, round the knuckles. Temporarily assemble the hinge leaves with the pins and check the action. With a chisel, carefully pare away stock that may still need to be removed. When you're satisfied that the hinges work properly, remove the pins to disassemble the leaves.

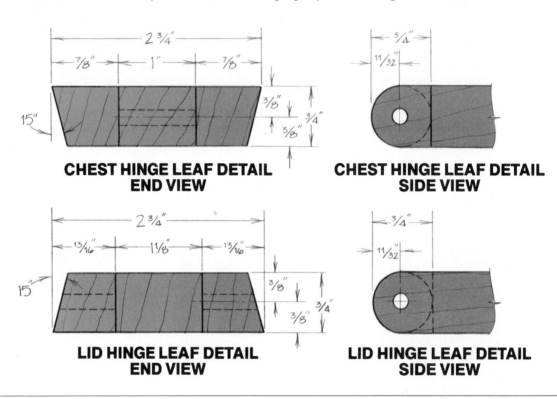

**CHEST HINGE LEAF DETAIL
END VIEW**

**CHEST HINGE LEAF DETAIL
SIDE VIEW**

**LID HINGE LEAF DETAIL
END VIEW**

**LID HINGE LEAF DETAIL
SIDE VIEW**

5 **Cut the bevels in the edges of the hinge leaves and the dovetail slots in the side and the lid.** Lay out the shape of the hinge leaves on the stock, as shown in the *Hinge Layout*. Tilt the table of your band saw to 15°, and cut the bevel in the edge of the leaves, keeping the leaves to the *outside* of the blade. (See Figure 2.) Cut a little wide of the layout line, and don't sand off the saw marks just yet.

Note: In our instructions and our drawings, we specify that the edge of the leaves should be beveled at 15°. This is because most dovetail router bits are angled at 15°. You should, however, check your bit before you cut or sand the bevels — the angle might be slightly different. If it is, use that angle instead.

From ¼″-thick tempered hardboard, cut two templates, as shown in the *Lid Hinge Slot Template Layout* and the *Chest Hinge Slot Template Layout,* to help you rout the dovetail slots in the chest parts. (Be sure that these templates are large enough to clamp them securely to the stock without the clamps interfering with the router.) To rout a slot, clamp one of these

2/Tilt your band saw table 15°, and cut the beveled edges of the leaves. Keep the stock to the outside of the blade.

templates to the appropriate chest part, with the open end of the template flush to the edge of the stock. Note that the slots in the back side are cut on the *outside* of the board, and the slots in the lid are cut on the *inside*.

Fit a ⁷⁄₁₆″ guide bushing in the router's baseplate and a ½″ dovetail bit in its collet. Adjust the depth of cut so that the bit will cut a ⅜″-deep recess in the wood when the base of the router is resting on top of the template. Keeping the guide bushing pressed firmly against the edge of the template, rout a dovetail slot around the perimeter. (See Figure 3.) Then rout out the waste, moving the router from side to side. (See Figure 4.) When the slot is complete, remove the template.

3/To rout the dovetail slots for the wooden hinges in the chest and lid, use a guide bushing and a template. The bushing is attached to the bit opening in the router's baseplate. The bushing has a hole through which the bit projects, but the hole is surrounded by a lip that rides against the edge of the template.

4/Keep the bushing pressed against the edge of the template and the base of the router flat on the face of the template.

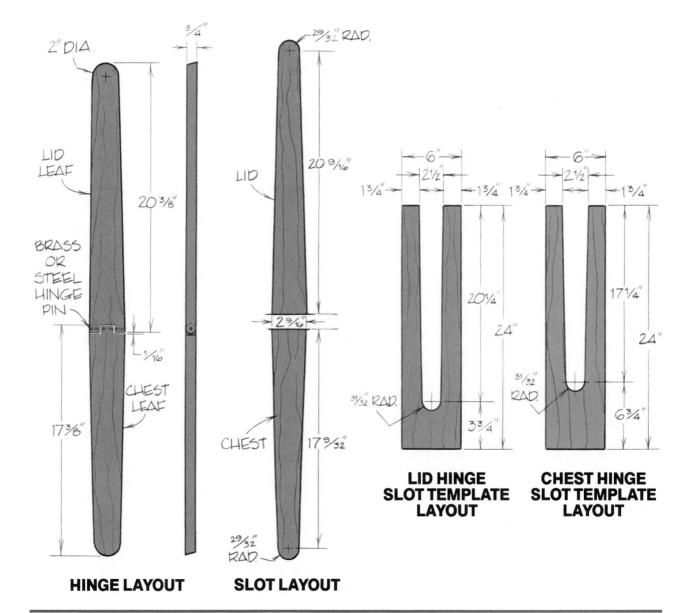

HINGE LAYOUT   **SLOT LAYOUT**

LID HINGE SLOT TEMPLATE LAYOUT   **CHEST HINGE SLOT TEMPLATE LAYOUT**

Carefully fit the hinge leaves to the slots by sanding away the saw marks and removing little bits of stock here and there around the edges, until they fit perfectly.

This will take some patience to achieve the precise fit you need. A disc sander, with the worktable tilted at 15°, helps make the job easier. (See Figure 5.)

TRY THIS! When you have "rough fit" a leaf to a slot and are wondering where you should remove stock to get a better fit, rub pencil lead on the inside edge of the slot. Use a #2 pencil, and rub it on heavily. Slide the leaf in the slot and tap the end lightly with a hammer. When you pull the leaf out again, the portions that are rubbing in the edge of the slot will be darkened by the pencil lead. Sand the dark areas off and repeat until you get a perfect fit.

5/A disc sander will help you accurately fit the leaves to the slots. Tilt the worktable to 15°, to match the bevel on the edge of the leaves.

6 Finish sand the parts of the chest.

Finish sand the individual parts of the chest. Be careful not to remove any more stock from the beveled edges of the wooden hinges. Be careful, too, not to round over surfaces that will join to other boards.

7 Assemble the chest and the tray.

Assemble the tray sides and ends with glue. Put the tray bottom in place in the groove as you assemble these parts, but *don't* glue the tray bottom in place. Let it float free in the grooves. Check that the tray is square as you clamp it up.

Assemble the chest sides and ends with glue. After you clamp it up, turn it upside down and glue the bottom in the rabbets. The bottom will hold the chest square while the glue dries. If you wish, reinforce the bottom glue joints with 4d finishing nails. Drive these nails through the bottom and into the sides and ends vertically so they won't show.

While the bottom is facing up, attach the feet to the bottom with glue and #8 x 1¼" flathead wood screws. Counterbore and countersink the screws so the heads will be just a little below the surface of the wood. This will keep the metal screws from scratching your floor.

8 Hinge the lid to the chest.

Slide the hinge leaves into their respective dovetail slots. *Do not* glue the leaves in place. Since the grain direction of the lid and the side run perpendicular to the grain direction of the leaves, the leaves must be free in their slots. This will allow the lid and the side to expand and contract slightly with changes in temperature and humidity. To keep the leaves from sliding out of their slots, hold each leaf in place with a single #8 x ¾" flathead wood screw. Place these screws near the knuckles, and drive them from *inside* the chest so they won't be seen.

If you are using metal hinges, attach the hinges so that the side leaves are on the outside of the chest and the lid leaves are on the inside — the same as the wooden hinges. This is a traditional arrangement for blanket chest hinges. It keeps the top free of hardware so that if you want to use the chest as a bench, you won't find yourself sitting on the knuckle of a hinge or the head of a screw.

Note: The leaves of the wooden hinges serve a double purpose. In addition to hinging the lid to the chest, they help to keep the lid from warping. If you use metal hinges, you should make two or three wooden cleats ¾" x 1½" x 18" to keep the lid true. Attach these to the underside of the lid with wood screws in *slotted* holes. (The slots allow the lid to expand and contract.) *Do not* glue them in place.

9

Finish the completed chest. Disassemble the lid from the chest. Finish sand any parts that may still need it, then apply a finish to the chest, inside and out. Be sure to put as many coats of finish on the inside as the outside. If you don't, one side will absorb or release moisture faster than the other, the wood will warp, and the chest will become distorted.

10

Line the chest with cedar. This step should be done last, *after* the chest is finished. The reason is that you don't want to finish the cedar. This would seal in the scent and destroy its value as a bug repellent.

Cedar "closet lining" comes in two forms — in strips of solid wood or in a chipboard panel. Whichever form you choose, the method of attaching it to the inside of the chest is the same. Just tack it in place with wire brads. You may want to glue it in place with contact cement, but this is not necessary.

When the cedar is in place, attach the runners to the sides with glue and #8 x 1¼″ flathead wood screws. The rabbet in the runners fits over the top edge of the side linings, as shown in the *End View* and the *Runner Joinery Detail.* Counterbore and countersink the screws, then cover the heads with plugs.

Note: You may apply a finish to the runners when you finish the other parts of the chest, but this isn't necessary. The sliding action of the tray will wear the finish away; instead, apply several coats of paste wax.

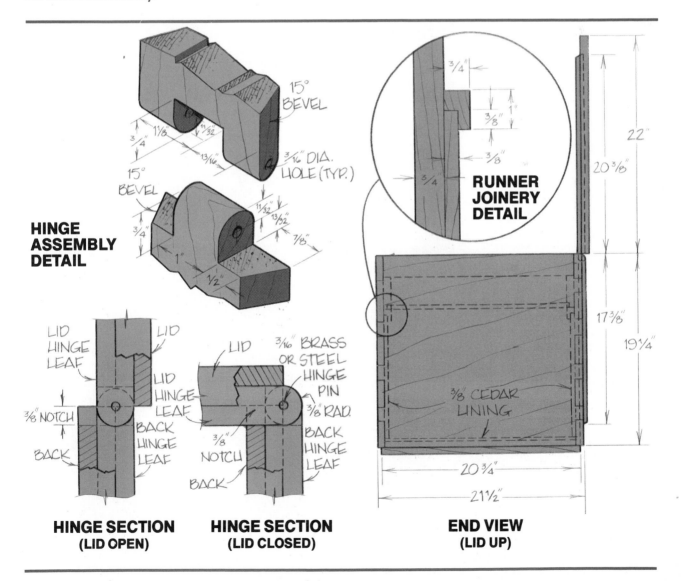

Classic Television Stand

It used to be a simple table — something to hold the television at eye level. Now a television stand has to provide space for a VCR and storage for video-tapes, remote controls, and all the paraphernalia you need to watch the tube.

This project is made in much the same manner as a traditional chest of drawers, with the exception of an open shelf that has been substituted for the top drawer. It's designed with simple, classic case construction. The drawers rest on web frames; the frames and the shelf are mounted in dadoes cut in the sides. Once assembled, the case is mounted on a simple frame-type base.

The design is classic, too — and easily changed if it doesn't suit your tastes. As shown here, the molded edges and the fretwork base are typical of many Chippendale chests made by colonial cabinetmakers in the mid-eighteenth century. The eastern white pine and the light finish make it an informal piece, equally at home in both country and classic settings. To adapt the design to other styles, simply change the molding, fretwork, or materials. ❁

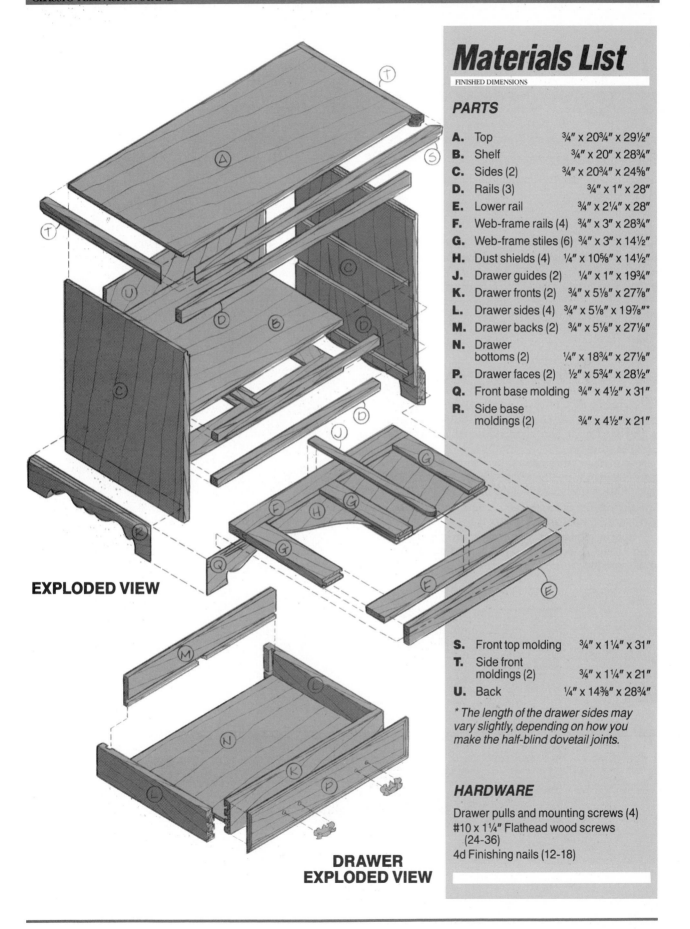

EXPLODED VIEW

**DRAWER
EXPLODED VIEW**

Materials List

FINISHED DIMENSIONS

PARTS

A.	Top	¾" x 20¾" x 29½"
B.	Shelf	¾" x 20" x 28¾"
C.	Sides (2)	¾" x 20¾" x 24⅝"
D.	Rails (3)	¾" x 1" x 28"
E.	Lower rail	¾" x 2¼" x 28"
F.	Web-frame rails (4)	¾" x 3" x 28¾"
G.	Web-frame stiles (6)	¾" x 3" x 14½"
H.	Dust shields (4)	¼" x 10⅝" x 14½"
J.	Drawer guides (2)	¼" x 1" x 19¾"
K.	Drawer fronts (2)	¾" x 5⅛" x 27⅞"
L.	Drawer sides (4)	¾" x 5⅛" x 19⅞"*
M.	Drawer backs (2)	¾" x 5⅛" x 27⅛"
N.	Drawer bottoms (2)	¼" x 18¾" x 27⅛"
P.	Drawer faces (2)	½" x 5¾" x 28½"
Q.	Front base molding	¾" x 4½" x 31"
R.	Side base moldings (2)	¾" x 4½" x 21"
S.	Front top molding	¾" x 1¼" x 31"
T.	Side front moldings (2)	¾" x 1¼" x 21"
U.	Back	¼" x 14⅜" x 28¾"

** The length of the drawer sides may
vary slightly, depending on how you
make the half-blind dovetail joints.*

HARDWARE

Drawer pulls and mounting screws (4)
#10 x 1¼" Flathead wood screws
   (24-36)
4d Finishing nails (12-18)

1 **Cut all parts to size.** To build this project, you'll need approximately 24 board feet of cabinet-grade lumber, 14 board feet of "utility" lumber, and a half sheet (4′ x 4′) of ¼″ plywood. Use the cabinet-grade lumber to make the parts that *show* on the completed project — top, sides, shelf, moldings, drawer faces, and so on. Make the web frames and drawer boxes — those

parts that *don't show* — from utility lumber. Use the plywood for the dust shields, drawer bottoms, and back.

Glue up the wide stock you need for the sides, top, and shelf. Cut all the parts, except the top and the base moldings, to the sizes shown in the Materials List. It's best to cut the moldings *after* you've made the case so that you can custom-fit them to the assembly.

2 **Make the joinery for the web-frame parts.** Using either a router or a dado cutter, cut ¼″-wide, ⅜″-deep grooves in *one* edge of the web-frame rails and the outside web-frame stiles. Cut grooves

in *both* edges of the inside web-frame stiles. Using the same tool you used to make the grooves, cut matching tongues in the ends of the stiles.

3 **Assemble the web frames.** Dry assemble the web-frame rails, stiles, and dust shields to check the fit. When you're satisfied that the parts fit properly, dismantle the frames and reassemble them with glue. *Do not* glue the shields in place; let them float in their grooves.

As you clamp the parts of the frames together, carefully check that the frames are square and *flat*. If there is a little bit of slop in the tongue-and-groove joints, or if you tighten the clamps a bit too tight, the rails may twist so that the frames are no longer flat.

After the glue cures, attach the drawer guides to the frames. Slightly round the front ends of the guides with a rasp and file. Then glue them to the frames so that they

TRY THIS! Wipe off excess glue that squeezes out between the joints with a wet rag. The rag must be wet enough to completely dissolve the glue, so that no trace of it remains on the surface of the wood. This will raise the grain slightly, but it won't hurt the wood — and it will save you a lot of work later on.

are centered on the middle stile, as shown in the *Web-Frame Layout.*

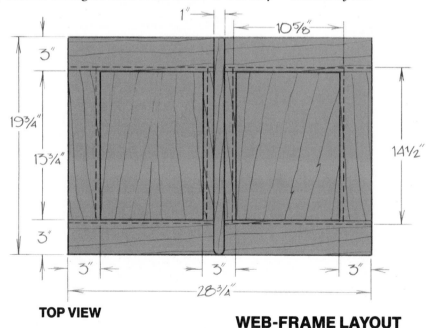

TOP VIEW

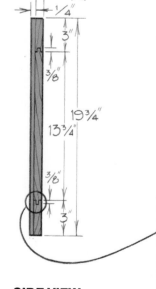

WEB-FRAME LAYOUT   **SIDE VIEW**

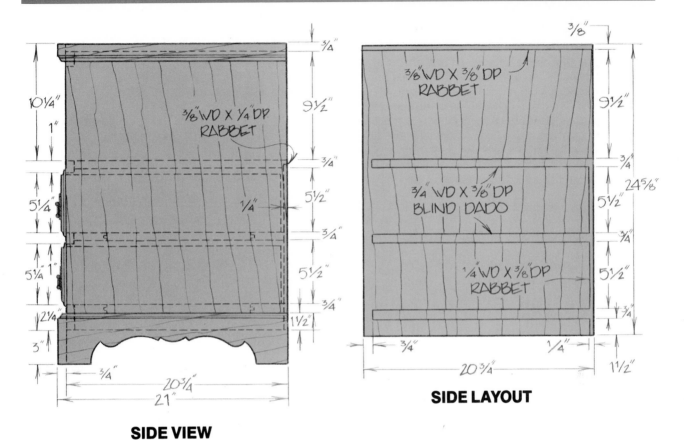

SIDE VIEW

SIDE LAYOUT

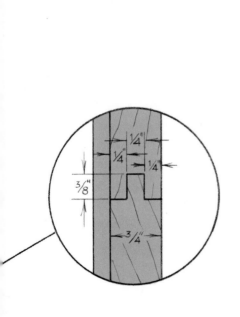

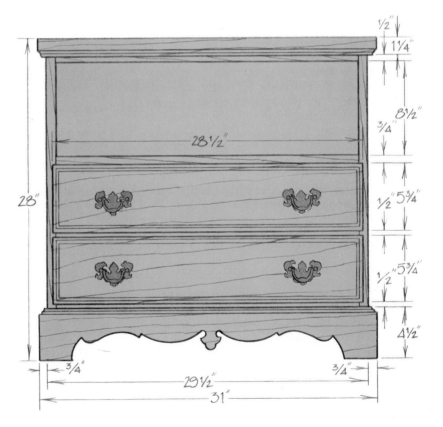

FRONT VIEW

4

Make the case joinery in the sides and the top. Using a router, cut the dadoes and the rabbets in the sides, as shown in the *Side Layout*. When you cut the ⅜″-wide, ⅜″-deep rabbet in the upper edges of the sides, also cut matching rabbets in the left and right edges of the top. When you assemble the case, these rabbets will interlock, as shown in the *Top-to-Side Joinery Detail*. After you rout all the joinery, square the ends of the blind dadoes in the sides with a chisel.

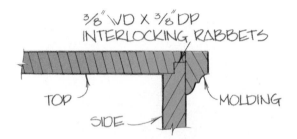

TOP-TO-SIDE JOINERY DETAIL

5

Finish sand the parts of the case. Scrape and sand the top, sides, and shelf. Be careful not to round over edges or corners that join other parts.

6

Assemble the case. Dry assemble the case parts and the web frames to check the fit. When you're satisfied that all the parts fit properly, dismantle the case. Reassemble the top, shelf, sides, and web frames with glue and screws.

Apply glue to the top and the shelf all along the adjoining surfaces. But only apply glue to the first 2″-3″ of the edges of the web frames (nearest the front of the case). *This is important!* Most of the web frame must be allowed to float in the stop dadoes so that the sides can expand and contract with changes in temperature and humidity. This is standard practice when assembling cases. The grain direction of the frame stiles opposes the grain of the sides. If the two parts were glued together, the stiles would inhibit the movement of the sides, and the case would warp.

Reinforce the frame-to-side glue joints by driving wood screws at an angle through the web frames and into the sides. (See Figure 1.) Once again, only drive these screws near the front edge of the case. Do not drive them all along the length of the dado joints.

Attach the rails to the top, shelf, and web frame with glue. Note that the rails attach to the *front edges* of the web frames and shelf and to the *underneath* of the top, flush with the front edge. Complete the case assembly by attaching the plywood back with glue and 4d finishing nails.

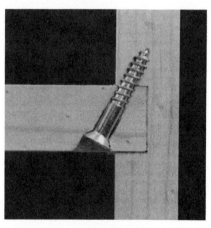

1/Reinforce the joints that hold the shelf and the web-frames to the sides with screws. Drive these screws at an angle, through the shelf or frame from inside the case and into the sides. This way, the screws will not be visible from the outside.

7

Shape the moldings and the drawer fronts. The shapes that we show for the moldings in the *Top Molding Profile* — the combined bead and cove — is known as a "bed" molding. This same shape is also shown on the edges of the drawer faces. You may use the bed molding shape, or any other that suits your fancy. Cut the edges of the molding and drawer front stock with a router or a shaper, then finish sand the stock.

Note: If you use a shaper to make the bed-molding profile, there are cutters available to create the shape in

TOP MOLDING PROFILE

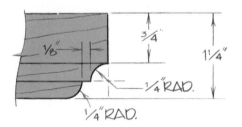

one pass. If you use a router, you'll have to cut the shape in two passes. Use a quarter-round bit to make the bead and a cove bit to cut the cove.

8

Attach the molding to the case. Do any necessary touch-up sanding on the case assembly. Then carefully measure and cut the top and base moldings. Miter the corners where the moldings join to each other.

Enlarge the *Front Base Molding Pattern* and the *Side Base Molding Pattern*. Trace these patterns on the base molding parts and cut out the shapes with a band saw or sabre saw. Sand the cut edges to remove the saw marks.

Attach the moldings to the case with glue and screws. Drive the screws from *inside* the case so that they won't show on the outside.

Remember that you glued only the front 2″-3″ of the web frames so that they wouldn't restrict the movement of the sides. The same consideration applies to the side moldings. The grain of the side moldings runs perpendicular to the grain of the sides. If the two parts are glued together, the case will warp or even break. To prevent this, only glue the front portion of each molding to

the side, applying glue just in the vicinity of the miter. Attach the remaining length of the molding with screws *only*. Drill oversize shaft holes for the screws so that the sides can expand and contract around the screws. (See Figure 2.)

2/So that the case can shrink and swell unrestricted, drill oversize holes in the sides for the screws that hold the moldings to the case. Wood "moves" up to ¼″ for every 12″ of width across the grain. If you space your screws every 6″, the shaft holes should be ⅛″ in diameter oversize.

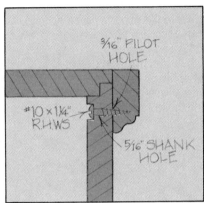

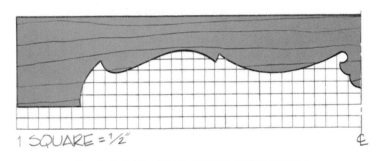

1 SQUARE = ½″

FRONT BASE MOLDING PATTERN

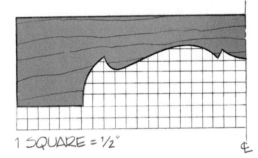

1 SQUARE = ½″

SIDE BASE MOLDING PATTERN

TRY THIS! The front base molding design includes a pendant in the center. These shapes are popular in both classic and country furniture designs, but they are also quite fragile. The wood grain runs side to side through the slender "neck" of the pendant, and it is likely to break off if you happen to kick it. To prevent this, glue a scrap block *behind* the pendant *before* you cut the shape. The grain of this block must run perpendicular to the grain of the molding so that it will strengthen the neck of the pendant.

9 **Cut the drawer joinery.** As shown in the *Drawer Top View, Side View,* and *Front View,* the drawers are assembled using traditional joints. Join the front to the sides with half blind dovetails. (If you don't have a dovetail jig and don't want to hand-cut the dovetails, you can also make a "lock" joint, as shown in Figure 3.) Join the back to the sides with dadoes. Then cut a groove for the bottom in the inside faces of the front, sides, and back.

Finally, cut a notch in the bottom edge of the drawer back, as shown in the *Drawer Back Layout.* This notch fits over the drawer guide on the web frame and keeps the drawer properly aligned as it slides in and out of the

3/If you don't want to make dovetails, you can join the drawer parts with lock joints. These can be made on a table saw with an ordinary combination blade.

case. To get it to fit properly, you may want to cut it a little small, then file it to the proper size *after* you completely assemble the drawer.

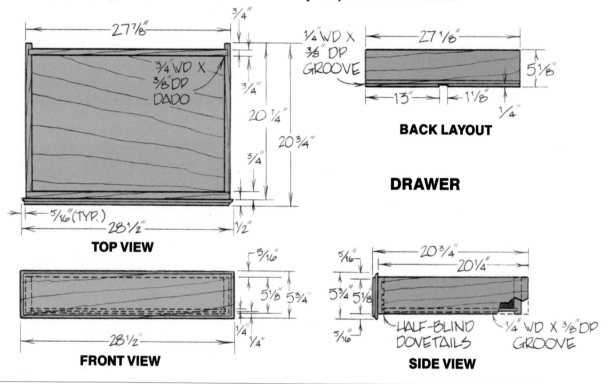

TOP VIEW

BACK LAYOUT

DRAWER

FRONT VIEW

SIDE VIEW

10 **Assemble the drawers.** Glue the drawer fronts, sides, and backs together, with the drawer bottoms in place. *Do not* glue the bottoms in the grooves; let them float. When the glue cures, check the fit of the drawers in the case. If necessary, remove a

little stock from the top or bottom edges of the drawers to improve the fit.

When you're satisfied with the fit, glue the faces to the drawer fronts. Drill holes through the faces and the fronts to attach the pulls to the drawers.

11 **Apply a finish to the completed television stand.** Do any necessary touch-up sanding, then apply a finish. Be sure to apply as many coats of finish to the inside of the case as you do to the outside — this will help prevent the case from warping.

When the finish dries, attach the pulls to the drawers and fit them to the case. You may also want to apply some paraffin to the bottom edges of the drawer parts to help them slide easily.

Bicycle Rack

A bicycle is a wonderful, economical form of transportation. It's great fun to ride. But the idle bicycle can be a nuisance.

In its natural state — with both wheels on the ground and one of those blocking a doorway — a bicycle at rest is annoying. When idle bicycles congregate, the annoyance becomes a burden. By some engineering miracle, two bikes in a driveway can take up as much room as a full-size car. Four bikes require as much space as a tractor-trailer rig. If that isn't problem enough, the bike you want to use always seems to be behind another. Move that bike and the whole lot of them falls down in a huge tangle of pedals, handlebars, spokes, and chains.

The solution is to get the bikes off the ground. If you hang them by one of their tire rims — vertically — they take up a third as much room. Space these hangers out properly, and you'll be able to fetch the bike you want when you want it, without having to wrestle the whole gang of them.

Materials List

FINISHED DIMENSIONS

PARTS

A. Top — ¾" x 15¼" x 48"
B. Braces (2) — ¾" x 14½" x 23¼"
C. Horizontal cleat — ¾" x 4" x 48"
D. Vertical cleats (2) — ¾" x 2¼" x 19¼"
E. Hanger bar — 1½" x 1½" x 48"

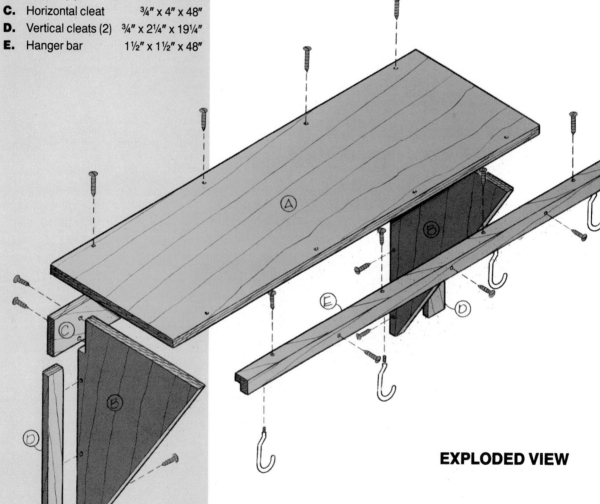

EXPLODED VIEW

HARDWARE

#10 x 1¼" Flathead wood screws
   (20-24)
¼" x 3" Lag screws and washers (5-6),
   or
¼" x 2½" Expandable lead shields and
   lag screws
Large, vinyl-covered screw hooks (4)

1

Adjust the design for your needs. As shown, this rack will hold four bicycles. If you have more or less than four bikes, adjust the size of the rack by extending or shrinking the length. The rack should be 12″ long for each bike you want to hang. If you extend the rack more than 48″ in length, add another brace in the middle. **Note:** If you have an odd number of bicycles, you'll have to position the middle brace 6″ to the left or the right of the true middle, so that it won't be in the way of the hanging bicycle.

2

Cut all parts to size. As we have designed it, you can make this rack from a half-sheet of ¾″ plywood and a 4′-long scrap of 2 x 2. Cut the parts to the sizes shown in the Materials List. Refer to the *Plywood Cutting Diagram* to see how you can get all the "one-by" parts out of a half-sheet.

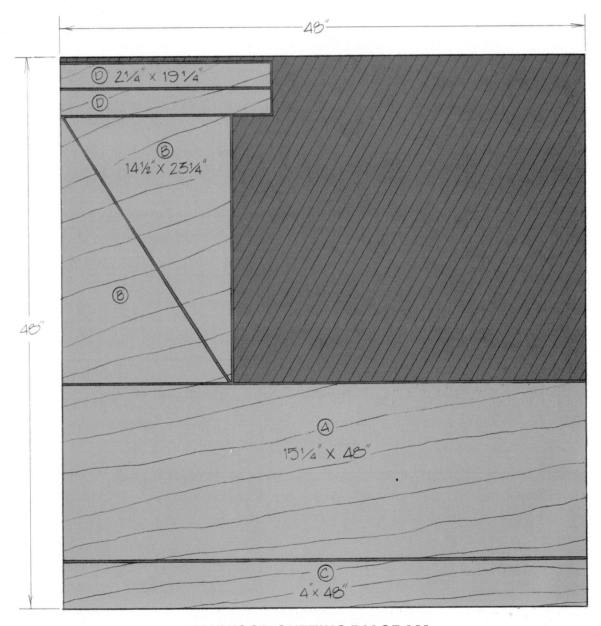

PLYWOOD CUTTING DIAGRAM

3

Cut a rabbet in the hanger bar. Cut a rabbet ¾″ deep and ¾″ wide along the hanger bar. Cut this joint on your table saw, making two passes over the blade. Adjust the blade and the rip fence, and make the first cut in the face of the stock. (See Figure 1.) Turn the board on its edge, and make the second cut. (See Figure 2.)

When cutting a rabbet in this manner, be careful of two things. First of all, use push sticks and featherboards to help keep your hands clear of the saw blade. This is especially important, since you have to remove the saw guard to make these cuts. Secondly, set up your saw so that you can make the second pass without leaving the waste in between the saw and the fence. If you make this mistake, the waste will kick back.

1/Make the rabbets in the hanger bar in two cuts. First, cut the face of the stock....

2/...then cut the edge. On the second cut, be careful not to leave the waste in between the saw blade and the rip fence. If you do, it will kick back.

4

Assemble the bike rack. Put the parts together with flathead wood screws. The parts can be assembled in almost any order, but you'll find it's easiest to attach the horizontal cleat to the braces *first*.

Next, attach the top, then the vertical cleats and the hanger bar. Finally, drill pilot holes for the screw hooks in the hanger bar, where shown in the *Front View* and *Side View,* and drive the screw hooks into the bar.

5

Finish the bike rack (optional). If you wish, you can paint or apply a finish to the rack. We suggest you do this *before* you mount the project.

Remove the screw hooks, and fill any visible voids in the plywood parts with wood putty. Sand the project, then apply a finish. After the finish dries, replace the hooks.

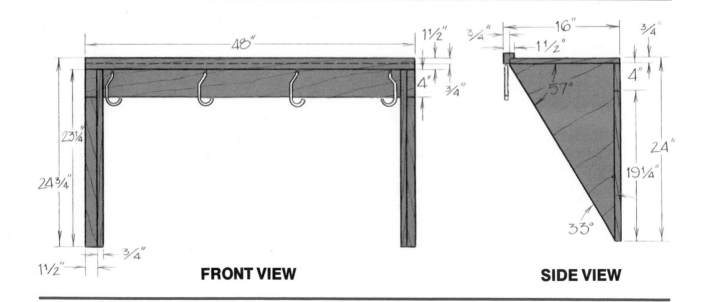

FRONT VIEW   **SIDE VIEW**

6

Mount the bike rack on the wall of your garage. Use the cleats to mount the bike rack to the wall of your garage. First, find the studs. Position each vertical cleat over a stud, if you can. Since the studs in most frame houses are either 16″ or 24″ on center, the vertical cleats on a 48″-long bike rack should line up with two of the studs. However, if they don't line up, use just the horizontal cleat to mount the rack. Just make sure that the horizontal cleat is attached to at least two different studs.

Drill pilot holes, and drive lag screws through the cleats into the studs. If you're mounting the project on a masonry wall, use expandable shields and lag screws.

Step-by-Step: Making Through Dovetails with a Jig

Until recently, through dovetail joints (such as those that join the parts of the *Blanket Chest*) were time-consuming to make. Most methods required a great deal of patient handwork. Now, however, there are two commercially made router jigs to help you make dovetails quickly and accurately. These are available from most mail-order woodworking catalogs, or you can write:

Leigh Industries
P.O. Box 357
Port Coquitlam, B.C.
Canada V3C 4K6

Keller & Co.
1327 I St.
Petaluma, CA 94952

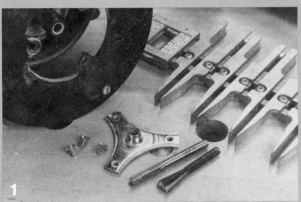

1 Both jigs work in a similar manner. *A guide bushing, which screws into the base plate of the router, rides against the jig, controlling the cut. The tails are cut using a dovetail router bit, and the pins using a straight bit.*

2 Always rout the tails first. *Use a scrap block to back up the workpiece and to help keep the wood from chipping or tearing.*

3 Make the pins last *so that you can fit them to the tails. To make the pins larger or smaller, move the fingers of the jig in or out, perpendicular to the face of the board.*

4 Dry assemble the completed pins and tails *to check the fit of the joint. If the router and the jig are both properly aligned, you shouldn't have to do any handwork to adjust the fit.*

Peg-Rail Storage Units

The peg rail may well be the most commonly recognized mark of the United Society of Believers in Christ's Second Reappearing, better known as the "Shakers." The Society used these elegant storage devices everywhere in their buildings. Entire rooms, more often than not, were lined with rows of Shaker pegs at eye level.

What we don't remember was that these mushroom-shaped pegs were just one part of a complete storage *system*. They weren't just for hanging clothes or an occasional ladder-back chair. In addition to the peg rails, the Shakers built shelves, cabinets, racks, and small storage units of all sorts that hung from the pegs. The advantage of this system was twofold. It allowed the Shakers to store all sorts of small items, using what would otherwise have been wasted wall space, and it allowed them to rearrange the storage easily when needs changed.

Many country folk copied this system. During the nineteenth century, it was not unusual for several walls in a farmhouse kitchen or bedroom to be lined with pegs and hung with peg-rail shelves and cabinets. These were usually more decorative than a good Shaker would have considered proper, but the purpose was the same. The hanging shelf and ventilated cabinet that you see here are typical of what you might have found.

While the decoration on both of these units is fairly involved, the construction is simple. This, too, is typical of country woodworking. Since a country craftsman's tools were usually limited, he kept the joinery basic. So have we: The shelves are assembled with dadoes, while the cabinet is put together with dadoes, grooves, and lap joints. ✹

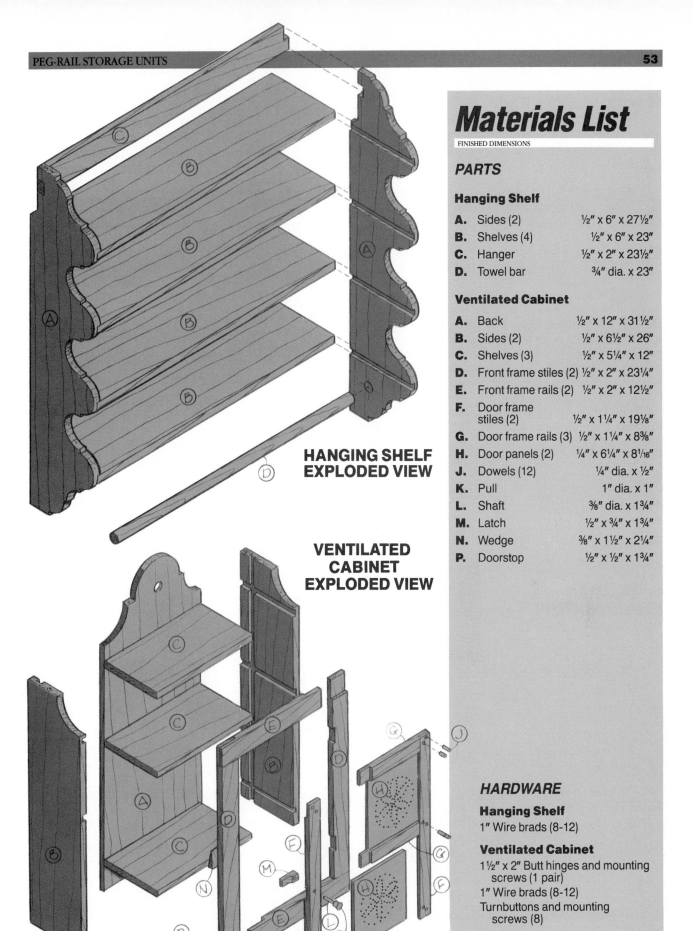

HANGING SHELF EXPLODED VIEW

VENTILATED CABINET EXPLODED VIEW

Materials List

FINISHED DIMENSIONS

PARTS

Hanging Shelf

A.	Sides (2)	½" x 6" x 27½"
B.	Shelves (4)	½" x 6" x 23"
C.	Hanger	½" x 2" x 23½"
D.	Towel bar	¾" dia. x 23"

Ventilated Cabinet

A.	Back	½" x 12" x 31½"
B.	Sides (2)	½" x 6½" x 26"
C.	Shelves (3)	½" x 5¼" x 12"
D.	Front frame stiles (2)	½" x 2" x 23¼"
E.	Front frame rails (2)	½" x 2" x 12½"
F.	Door frame stiles (2)	½" x 1¼" x 19⅛"
G.	Door frame rails (3)	½" x 1¼" x 8⅜"
H.	Door panels (2)	¼" x 6¼" x 8 1/16"
J.	Dowels (12)	¼" dia. x ½"
K.	Pull	1" dia. x 1"
L.	Shaft	⅜" dia. x 1¾"
M.	Latch	½" x ¾" x 1¾"
N.	Wedge	⅜" x 1½" x 2¼"
P.	Doorstop	½" x ½" x 1¾"

HARDWARE

Hanging Shelf

1" Wire brads (8-12)

Ventilated Cabinet

1½" x 2" Butt hinges and mounting screws (1 pair)

1" Wire brads (8-12)

Turnbuttons and mounting screws (8)

Making the Peg Rail

1 Assemble the peg rail.
If you're going to build a peg-rail storage system, the first thing you need is a peg rail. To make this, first cut a hardwood rail 4″ wide and as long as you need. You may want the rail to span the complete length of the wall; you may want it somewhat shorter. You might even want the rail to span several walls, in which case you'll need several pieces.

Note: The rails must be made of hardwood so that they will be strong enough to support the shelves and cabinets you intend to hang. If you make them from softwood, the peg holes will become elongated, and the pegs will gradually work loose. Elsewhere, you can use any sort of domestic wood — white pine would have been the preferred material of most country craftsmen for the shelves and cabinet.

Chamfer the edges of the rail, then drill stopped holes to accept the pegs. Space the holes 3½″ from the ends of the rails and 6″ apart, as shown in the *Peg Rail Exploded View*. Finish sand the rail, then glue pegs in the holes.

You can turn the Shaker pegs, if you want, but that will take a great deal of time, and it is tedious work after the first two or three. You can buy the pegs ready-made. Here are two mail-order sources:

Shaker Workshops
P.O. Box 1028
Concord, MA 01742

The Woodworker's Store
21801 Industrial Blvd.
Rogers, MN 55374

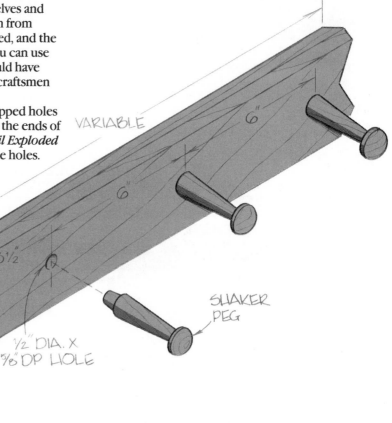

**PEG RAIL
EXPLODED VIEW**

VARIABLE

6″

6″

6″

3½″

4″

½″

45°
(TYP.)

¾″

½″ DIA. X
⅝″ DP HOLE

SHAKER
PEG

2 Paint or finish the peg rail.
Finish sand the assembled peg rail where needed, then apply a finish or paint. If you choose to paint the rail, use a milk paint, which was a traditional country finish. It can be applied either as an opaque coat or as a transparent stain.

3 Mount the peg rail on the wall.
Attach the peg rail to the wall at (or a little bit above) eye level. Secure the rail to the studs in the wall with wood screws. (Since this peg rail will support quite a bit of weight, it's important that it be attached directly to the frame of the house.) Counterbore the holes in the rail for these screws, then cover the screw heads with wooden plugs.

Making the Hanging Shelf

1 Cut the parts to size. To make the shelf, you'll need approximately 6 board feet of lumber and a 2′ length of ¾″-diameter dowel. Surface the lumber to ½″ thick. (The reason for the thin stock is to reduce the weight of the shelf. This, in turn, reduces the load on the peg rail.) Cut the stock and the dowel to the sizes shown in the Materials List.

2 Make the joinery in the sides and the hanger. Make the joinery in the sides *before* you cut the shapes. Using a router or a dado cutter, make ½″-wide, ¼″-deep dadoes for the shelves. Drill ¾″-diameter, ¼″-deep stopped holes to hold the towel bar. (See Figure 1.) Finally, cut notches in the upper back corners of the sides. Each side gets two notches, as shown in the *Side View*. First cut a long notch so that the sides will fit around the peg rail. Then cut a smaller notch (in the first notch!) for the hanger. Cut a matching tenon on each end of the hanger, as shown in the *Hanger-to-Back Assembly Detail*.

Note: As you cut the notches, you may realize that when the shelving unit is assembled, the end grain of the hanger will show. (The same is true of the lap joints in the ventilated cabinet — the end grain of the rails shows.) This construction was typical of country woodworking. End grain did not bother the country craftsman the way it bothers us because most country furniture was *painted* rather than stained or varnished. The end grain was camouflaged by the pigment.

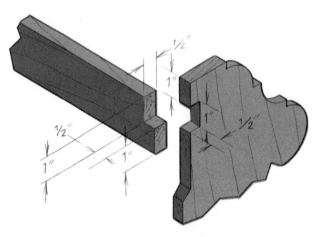

1/If you use a router to make the dadoes, you can cut both sides at the same time. Clamp the two parts to the workbench, side by side.

HANGER-TO-BACK ASSEMBLY DETAIL

3 Cut the shapes of the sides. Carefully lay out the shapes of the sides on the stock, following the *Side Layout*. Although this is a complex shape, you don't need to enlarge any patterns. You can draw the shapes with just a compass and a straightedge. Cut out the shapes with a band saw or a sabre saw.

TRY THIS! Since both sides are exactly the same, you can save some work by "pad" sawing the parts. Stack the sides together in a "pad" with the dadoes perfectly aligned and facing each other. Tack this pad together with a few small brads through the waste areas of the stock. Saw both parts at the same time.

4 **Finish sand the parts.** Sand or file away the saw marks from the cut edges of the sides. Finish sand all surfaces of all the parts. Be careful not to remove too much stock from the faces of the shelves. If you do, the shelves will be loose in their dadoes.

5 **Assemble the shelves.** Dry assemble the unit to make sure that the joints fit properly. When you're satisfied that they do, reassemble the parts with glue. Clamp the parts together, making certain that the sides are square to the shelves as you tighten the clamps.

After the glue cures, reinforce the dado joints that hold the top and bottom shelves with wire brads. Drive these brads in at an angle, from the top or bottom surfaces of the shelves and into the sides, so that they "hook" the parts together. (See Figure 2.) Set the heads of the brads below the surface of the wood with a sharp punch.

2/Make a simple jig to hold the brad at the correct angle by drilling a 1/16" hole in a scrap of 1/4"-thick stock. The hole is large enough so that you can lift the jig off over the brad once you've started it into the wood.

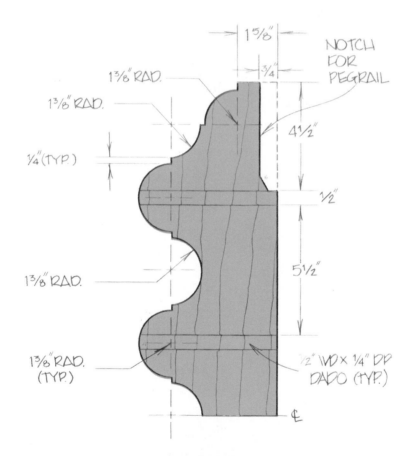

**HANGING SHELF
SIDE LAYOUT**

6 **Finish the completed shelves.** Fill the brad holes with putty or stick shellac, and do any necessary touch-up sanding on the assembled shelves. Then apply a finish according to your tastes.

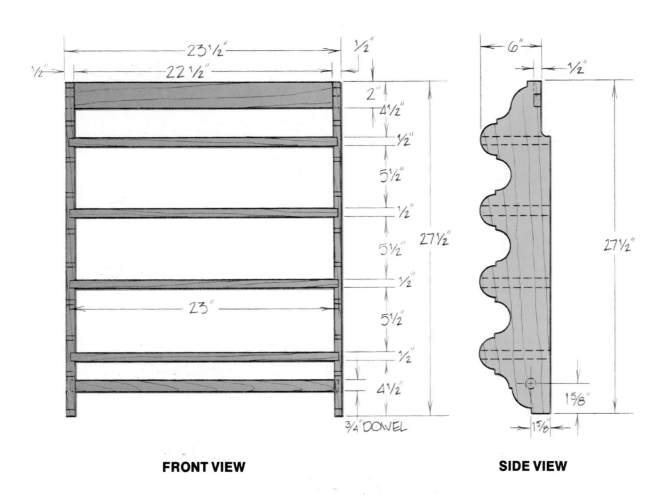

FRONT VIEW   **SIDE VIEW**

HANGING SHELF

Making the Ventilated Cabinet

1 **Cut the parts to size.** To make the cabinet, you'll need approximately 9 board feet of lumber. Surface 1 foot or so of this stock to ¼″ thick (enough to make the ventilated panels), then surface the rest of the lumber to ½″ thick. (Once again, the thin stock saves weight.) Cut all the parts to the sizes shown in the Materials List.

2 Cut the joinery in the sides, stiles, and rails.

Using a dado cutter or a router, make ½"-wide, ¼"-deep dadoes and grooves in the sides, as shown in the *Side Layout*. Notice that the sides of this cabinet *overhang the back* by ¾". (The sides of most cabinets are *flush* with the back.) The overhang compensates for the peg rail, allowing the cabinet to rest solidly against the wall as it hangs. Without it, the cabinet would stand out from the wall the same distance as the thickness of the peg rail; it might hang leaning slightly forward. Certainly, it would tend to rock back and forth if you brushed up against it.

To make the lap joints in the ends of the stiles and rails, you can use the same tool setup you used in making the dadoes. If you're using a dado cutter mounted in your table saw, cut each lap joint in several passes. Use a stop block to help gauge the last pass. (See Figure 3.)

If you're using a router, you can cut end laps in *adjoining* rails and stiles all at the same time. Clamp the parts

3/If you use your table saw and a dado cutter to make the lap joints, attach a stop block to your rip fence to help gauge the cuts. Without the block, the stock may bind between the fence and the cutter and kick back.

to your workbench so that the ends are flush, then clamp a straightedge across the parts to guide the router. Cut the joints in several passes. You can cut the middle laps in the door stiles using a variation on this method, but you'll need to use *two* straightedges to guide the router, one on each side of the lap.

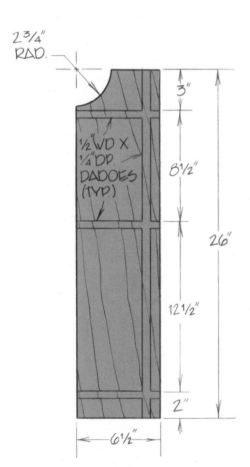

2¾" RAD.

3"

½" WD X ¼" DP. DADOES (TYP)

8½"

26"

12½"

2"

6½"

SIDE LAYOUT

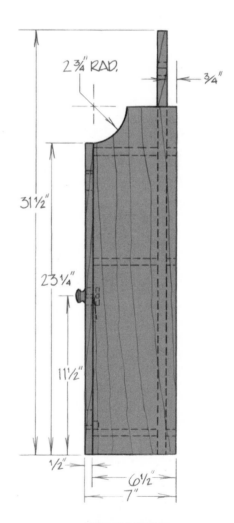

2¾" RAD.

¾"

31½"

23¼"

11½"

½"

6½"

7"

SIDE VIEW

3

Cut the shape of the back. Lay out the top portion of the back, as shown in the *Back Layout*. This is a shape similar to the one you used to make the sides of the hanging shelves. As before, there are no patterns to enlarge; all you need is a compass and a straightedge. Cut the back with a band saw or a sabre saw.

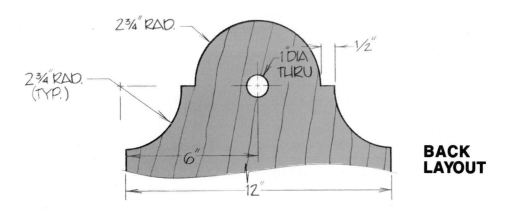

BACK LAYOUT

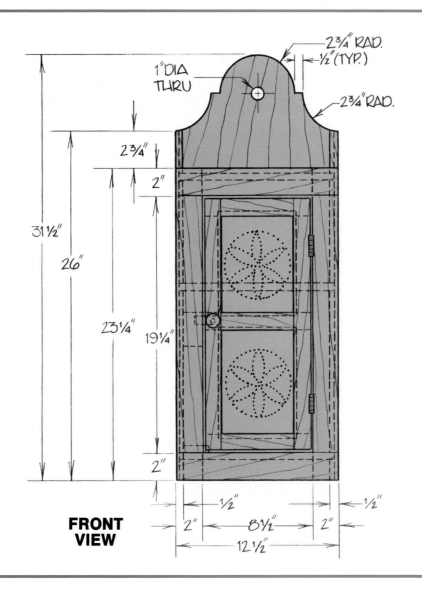

FRONT VIEW

4 *Make the design in the door panels.*

The wooden door panels are pierced with many small holes that form a traditional "hex star" design. (The six-pointed star was a symbol of good luck to many country folk.) Like all the designs in this project, this, too, can be laid out with basic drafting tools, following the steps in the *Hex Star Layout:*

One, draw a circle with a radius of 2¾″ in the center of the panel. *Two,* put the point of the compass on the circumference of the circle near the bottom edge of the panel. Draw an arc of the same radius that intersects the circle at two points. *Three,* move the point of the compass to one of these points of intersection and draw another arc. Repeat, until you have drawn six arcs. These will form a hex star. *Four,* draw a line from the center of the circle to a point on the circumference. Divide this line into ¼″ segments. *Five,* place the point of the compass at the center of the circle and draw "concentric arcs" that intersect the points on the line *and* the first six arcs. *Six,* continue until you have drawn ten sets of concentric arcs, spaced ¼″ apart.

Where the concentric arcs cross the arcs that make the hex star, drill ⅛″-diameter holes through the panel.

You can save yourself the trouble of drawing a second star by stacking the panels and drilling both at the same time. Hold the two together with masking tape until you've made all the holes.

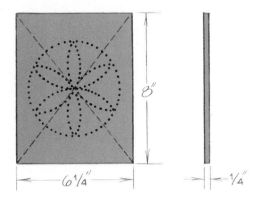

FRONT VIEW   **SIDE VIEW**

PANEL LAYOUT

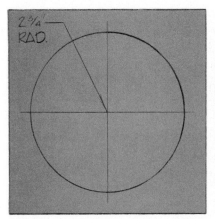

STEP 1.

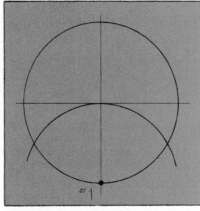

STEP 2.

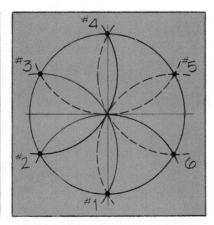

STEP 3.

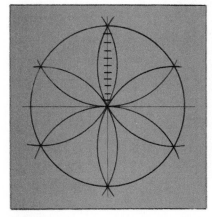

STEP 4.

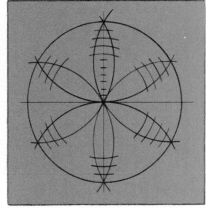

STEP 5.

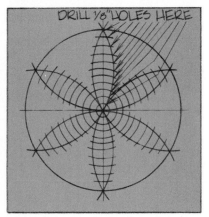

STEP 6.

HEX STAR LAYOUT

5 Finish sand all parts.

Finish sand all parts. Sand or file away the saw marks from the cut edges of the back. Finish sand all surfaces of all the parts. As before, do not remove too much stock from the faces of the shelves or the back, so that these parts will remain snug in their dadoes and grooves. Also, be careful not to round over the corners of any adjoining surfaces.

6 Assemble the frames.

Assemble the frames. Dry assemble the face and door frames to check the fit of the lap joints. When you're satisfied that the parts fit correctly, reassemble these frames with glue. Clamp the parts together, checking that the frames remain square as you tighten the clamps.

When the glue cures, reinforce the door frame joints with ¼″ dowels, as shown in the *Door Frame Layout*. The face frame needs no dowels. It will not see as much wear and tear as the door, and moreover, its joints will be reinforced by the cabinet structure.

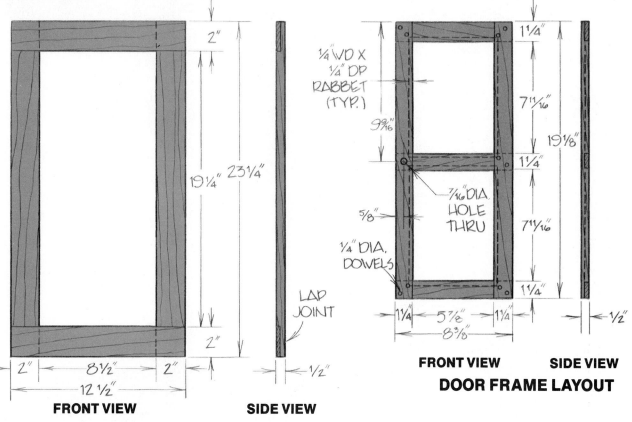

FRONT VIEW   **SIDE VIEW**

FACE FRAME LAYOUT

FRONT VIEW   **SIDE VIEW**

DOOR FRAME LAYOUT

7 Assemble the cabinet.

Assemble the cabinet. Dry assemble the sides, back, and shelves to check the fit of the joints, then reassemble the parts with glue. After the glue cures, reinforce the dado joints on the top and bottom shelves with wire brads. Drive these brads at an angle from the top or bottom surface of the shelves into the sides, hooking the parts together — as you did when you assembled the hanging shelves.

Glue the face frame onto the cabinet assembly. If you wish, you can reinforce this glue joint with splines or dowels, but as long as the two assemblies fit together well, it's not necessary. This is a small cabinet, and there is sufficient gluing surface to hold all the parts together. Before the glue dries, wipe off the excess with a wet rag. This little bit of water will not harm the wood.

8

Assemble the door. Using a rabbeting bit in your router, cut ¼″-wide, ¼″-deep rabbets on the inside edges of the door frame to hold the door panels. Square the corners where the rabbets meet with a sharp chisel. Place the door panels in these rabbets and secure them with turnbuttons. (See Figure 4.)

Drill a ⁷⁄₁₆″-diameter hole through the door frame where you want to put the pull and latch. (You can locate this latch *almost* anywhere on the door frame — just be certain that neither the shelves nor the turnbuttons interferes with its operation.) Drill a ⅜″-diameter hole through the latch near one end, and a ⅜″-diameter *stopped* hole in the back of the pull. "Thin out" a portion of the latch with a band saw or a scroll saw, as shown in the *Latch and Wedge Detail.*

Insert the shaft through the hole in the door frame, and glue the pull and the latch to either end. This assembly should be snug, but not too tight. You must be able to turn the pull and the latch easily.

4/Use turnbuttons to secure the panels in the door frame. These are available in the "screen door hardware" section of most hardware stores. Be careful to place the turnbuttons so that they won't hit a shelf when you close the door.

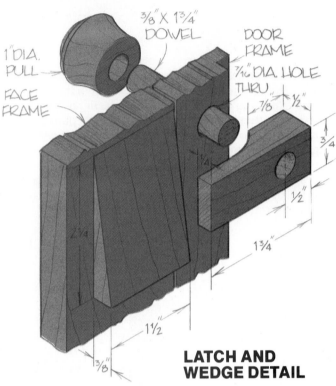

LATCH AND WEDGE DETAIL

9

Hang the door in the cabinets. Test fit the door to the cabinet and mark the position of the wedge. Glue the wedge and the doorstop to the inside surface of the face frame.

With a chisel, mortise the face frame and the door frame for the hinges. Mount the door on the cabinet, so that there is a ¹⁄₁₆″ clearance all around the door.

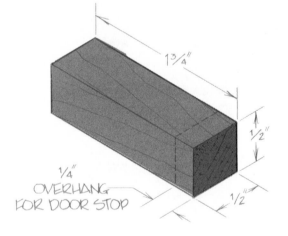

DOOR STOP DETAIL

10

Finish the completed cabinet. Remove the door from the cabinet and the panels from the door frame. Remove all hardware and set aside. Apply a finish to all wooden parts. Be careful to

apply as many coats of finish to the inside of the cabinet as you do to the outside. This will help keep the parts of the cabinet from warping.

Firewood Box

If you have a fireplace in your home, then you understand that firewood presents a unique set of storage problems. First of all, the storage is always short-term. You bring the wood inside, keep it for a few hours, then burn it up — similar to a bag of potato chips. Or your paycheck. Secondly, the wood is filthy. Though the average life of a piece of firewood inside your home is brief, it seems to shed its weight in bark and sawdust before you burn it up. And finally, firewood comes in two assorted sizes — logs and kindling. There is a frustrating (but inescapable) law of pyrotechnics that states: If you only have one pile of firewood, then the size of the wood on the top of the pile will be exactly the opposite of the size you need.

The firewood box you see here will solve all of these storage problems. The entire lid opens, so that you can easily get the firewood in and out. It's completely enclosed, to prevent the spread of firewood droppings. And there are two compartments inside the box: one to store logs, and the other to store newspapers and matches. There's even a third compartment, under the newspaper bin, to store kindling for starting your fires. ✳

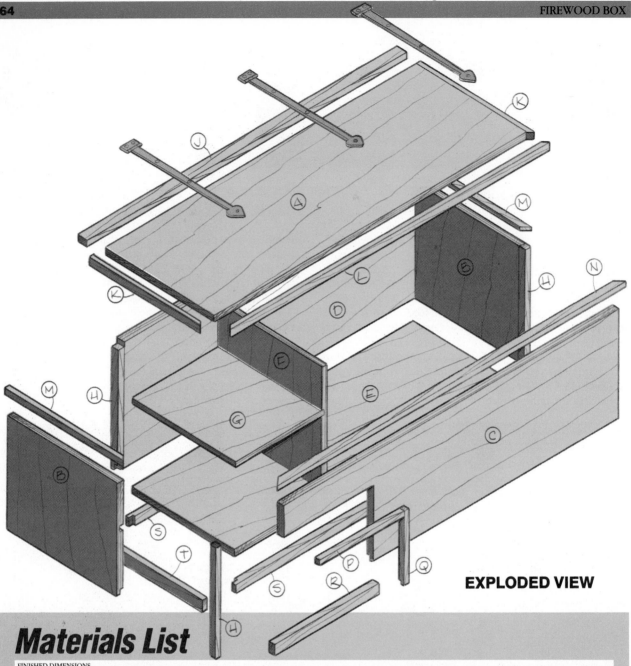

EXPLODED VIEW

Materials List

FINISHED DIMENSIONS

PARTS

A.	Lid	¾″ x 17″ x 48″
B.	Sides (2)	¾″ x 15¾″ x 16¼″
C.	Front	¾″ x 15¾″ x 46½″
D.	Back	¾″ x 16¼″ x 46½″
E.	Bottom	¾″ x 16¼″ x 46½″
F.	Divider	¾″ x 14½″ x 16¼″
G.	Kindling bin bottom	¾″ x 13¾″ x 16¼″
H.	Corner posts (4)	¾″ x ¾″ x 15¾″
J.	Top	¾″ x 1¼″ x 49″

K.	Side lid trim (2)	½″ x ¾″ x 17½″
L.	Front lid trim	½″ x ¾″ x 49″
M.	Side box trim (2)	½″ x ¾″ x 17¾″
N.	Front box trim	½″ x ¾″ x 48″
P.	Top bin trim	¾″ x ¾″ x 13″
Q.	Side bin trim	¾″ x ¾″ x 10″
R.	Bottom bin trim	¾″ x 1¼″ x 13″
S.	Base front/ back (2)	¾″ x 1½″ x 47¼″
T.	Base sides (2)	¾″ x 1½″ x 17″

HARDWARE

Decorative wrought-iron T-hinges and mounting screws (3)

4d Finishing nails (¼ lb.)

#10 x 1½″ Flathead wood screws (36-48)

1

Cut all parts to size. To make this firewood box, you'll need one sheet of ¾" plywood and a 1 x 12, 4' long. You can use ordinary fir plywood or something more attractive. The firewood box, as it's pictured here, was made of pine plywood, a so-called hardwood plywood whose face veneers are flinch-cut rather than rotary cut. You can also use birch, cherry, walnut and other quality plywoods. Of the hardwood plywoods we just mentioned, the only one that lumberyards and building centers commonly carry is birch. They will, however, special-order other plywoods for you if you ask.

Cut the parts to the sizes shown in the Materials List. Refer to the *Plywood Cutting Diagram* to see how you can get all the plywood parts out of a single 4' x 8' sheet. When you cut the front, cut out a section 13¾" wide and 10" high from the lower left front corner (as you look at the box from the front). This will become the opening for the kindling compartment.

Note: Since this box will get considerable use and abuse, consider making the corner posts, top, and trim parts from a tough hardwood, such as oak or rock maple. Hardwood trim will wear better, especially when you drop a log against the side of the box.

> *TRY THIS!* Keep a 4' x 8' sheet of fiber underlayment (sometimes called "builder's board") to help cut up full sheets of plywood. Lay the underlayment on the floor of your shop, and the plywood on top of it. Adjust the depth of cut on your circular saw so that it cuts through the plywood and about ⅛" into the underlayment. Cutting sheet materials flat on the floor is a lot easier (and a lot safer) than trying to support them between two sawbucks.

2

Cut the rabbets in the bottom corners of the box parts. Cut ⅜"-wide, ½"-deep rabbets in the bottom edge of the back, sides, front, and bottom bin trim. You can cut these joints with a dado cutter mounted in your table saw, or a router and a piloted rabbeting bit.

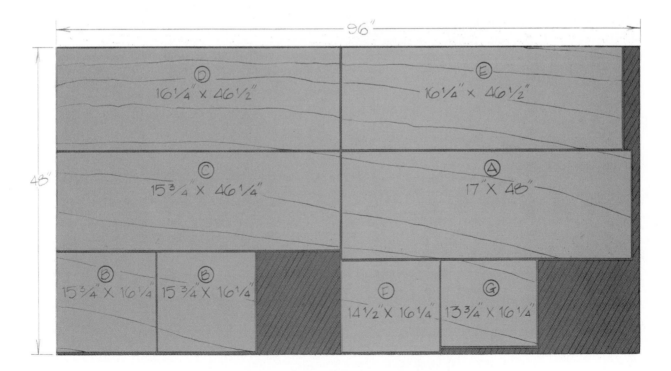

PLYWOOD CUTTING DIAGRAM

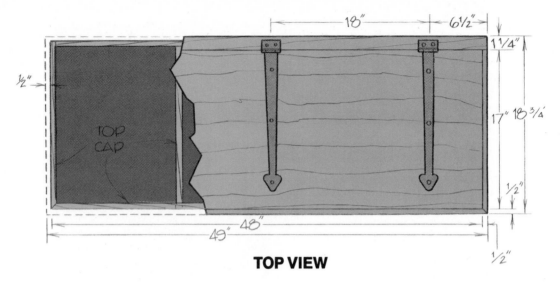

TOP VIEW

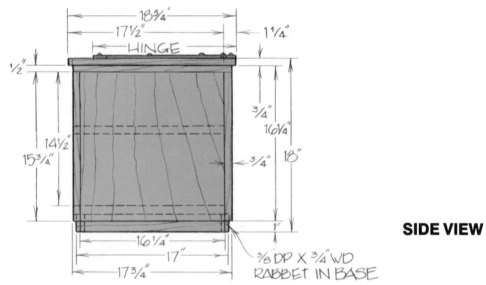

SIDE VIEW

⅜ DP X ¾" WD
RABBET IN BASE

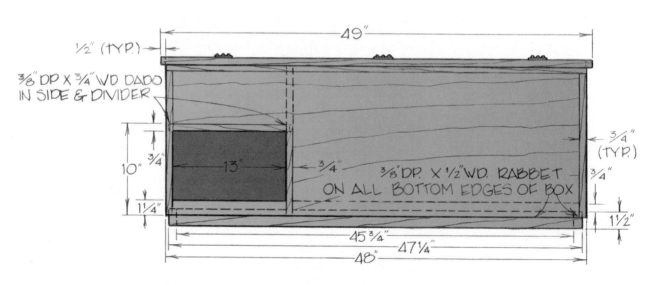

FRONT VIEW

3 Cut the rabbets in the base front and back.

Cut the rabbets in the ends of the base front and back, as shown in the *Base Front/Back Detail*. Once again, you can use either a dado cutter or a router to make these joints.

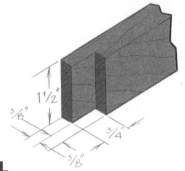

BASE FRONT/BACK DETAIL

4 Cut the notches in the bottom corner of the corner posts.

The corner posts must be notched at the bottom to fit over the base assembly, as shown in the *Corner Post Detail*. The easiest way to make these notches is to rough them out with a drill press, then clean them up with a *very* sharp chisel. Drill a ⅜″-diameter hole, ½″ deep in the end of each post, near one corner. Using the chisel, pare away stock from the sides of this hole until you have a rectangular notch, ⅜″ x ⅜″ x ½″. (See Figures 1 and 2.)

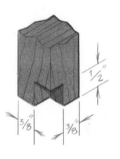

CORNER POST DETAIL

1/To make the notches in the corner posts, first drill a ⅜″-diameter, ½″-deep stopped hole in the bottom end of each post, near the corner of the stock. You must use a drill press and clamp the wood firmly to the table so that it doesn't move. If you have a ⅜″ Forstner bit, use it for this operation.

2/After you drill the hole, square the sides with a chisel. This chisel should be very sharp to cut the end grains cleanly.

TRY THIS! How do you know when a chisel is sharp? Look at the cutting edge straight on, in a bright light. If you see a shiny "line of light" reflected from any portion of the edge like the chisel on the left, then it needs sharpening. The edge of a properly sharpened chisel, like the one on the right, will not reflect light.

5

Cut the dadoes to hold the newspaper bin bottom. With a dado cutter or a router, cut ¾"-wide, ⅜"-deep dadoes in the left side (as you look at the box from the front) and the divider. These dadoes must be 4½" from the top edge of both parts, as shown in the *Divider Layout*.

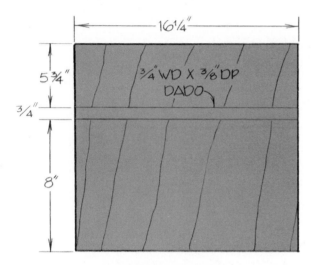

DIVIDER LAYOUT

TRY THIS! To keep plywood from tearing out or chipping when you cut a dado or a rabbet, carefully lay out the joint on the stock and score the lines with a scratch awl or a marking knife. This cuts the grain fibers at the edge of the joint so that the cutter will not "lift" them as it passes by. The dado on the left was made without scoring the joint, and the dado on the right was scored before it was cut. As you can see, by scoring the joint first, you get a much cleaner edge.

6

Assemble the base. Join the base front and back to the base sides with glue and screws. Counterbore and countersink the screws, then cover the heads with screw plugs. Sand the plugs flush with the surface of the wood.

7

Assemble the box. Attach the corner posts to the box sides with glue and screws. As you did when assembling the base, counterbore and countersink all screws. Make sure that the notches in the corner posts line up with the rabbets in the sides. Join the side/post assembly to the front, back, and bottom with glue and screws. Finally, attach the divider and the newspaper bin bottom inside the box with glue and screws. Cover the heads of the screws with screw plugs, and sand the plugs flush with the surface of the wood.

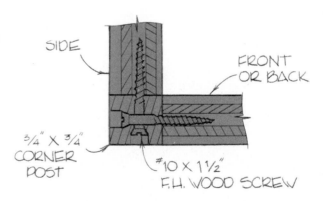

CORNER JOINERY DETAIL

8

Attach the box to the base. Turn the box assembly over, upside down. Glue the base assembly in place, inside the rabbets and the notches in the box parts. Reinforce the glue joints with 4d finishing nails. Drive these nails at a fairly steep angle, from inside the base assembly, as shown in the *Case/Base Joinery Detail*. If you don't drive them at an angle, they may come through the outside of the box.

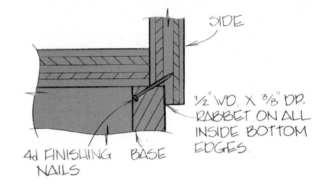

SIDE

½" WD. X ⅜" DP. RABBET ON ALL INSIDE BOTTOM EDGES.

4d FINISHING NAILS

BASE

CASE/BASE JOINERY DETAIL

9

Attach the trim to the box and the lid. Attach the trim parts to the box assembly and the lid with glue and finishing nails. Set the nails, then cover the heads with wood putty.

BOTTOM BIN TRIM DETAIL

¾"

11¼"

½"

⅜"

10

Finish sand the box and lid. Finish sand both the lid assembly and box/base assembly. If necessary, "true up" the trim and the corner posts, so that the outside edges are flush with the outside surfaces of the plywood parts.

11

Hinge the lid to the box. Attach the lid to the box with three decorative wrought-iron T-hinges. These hinges are available at many hardware stores and building-supply stores. They can usually be found with gate hardware. If not, you may have to place a special order. You can also order them from:

The Renovator's Supply
Renovator's Old Mill
Millers Falls, MA 01349

12

Apply a finish to the completed firewood box. Once you're satisfied with the lid and the action of the hinges, detach the lid from the box and remove the hinges. Finish sand any parts that may still need it, then apply a finish to the completed firewood box and lid. When the finish dries, re-attach the lid and the hinges to the box.

Stacking Boxes

For versatile, economic storage you just can't beat the box. As simple and as mundane as it may be, a box solves most storage problems very neatly. It will store almost anything — as long as that "anything" is smaller than the box.

A box can be used in different positions for different types of storage. Resting on its bottom, an open-top box makes a bin. When turned on its side, the box becomes a shelf or an open cabinet. If you make more than one box, you can stack them on top of each other and side by side to make an entire storage system.

The boxes you see here offer several additional advantages over ordinary storage boxes. They're strong enough to be stacked five or six deep, yet they're light and easy to handle. They are ventilated so that clothes and other fabric items won't smell musty after they have been stored for a time. Finally, the boxes are simple and economical to build. They are designed for "mass production," so that you can set up your tools and turn out a dozen or so in a weekend. ✸

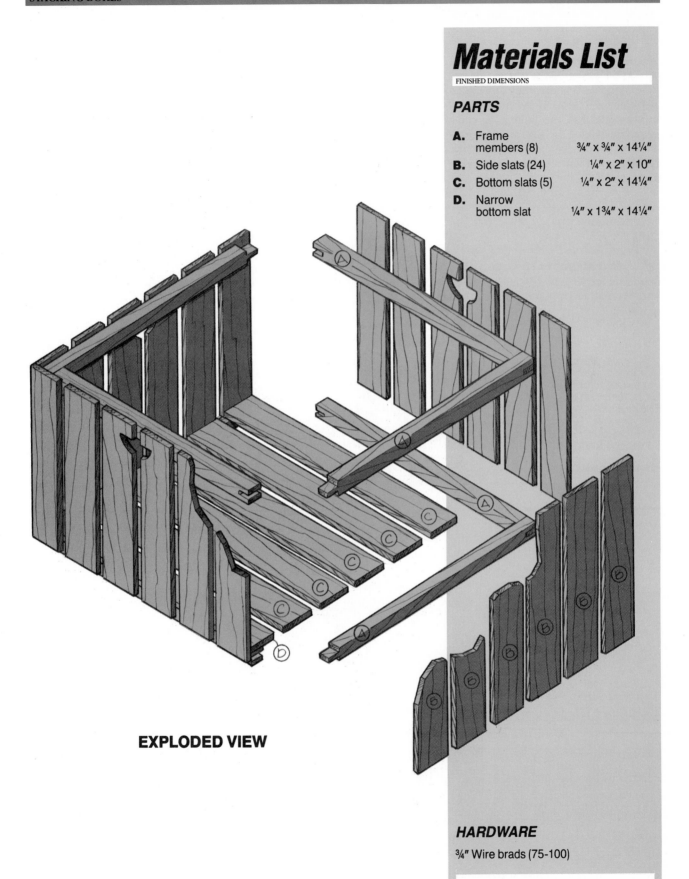

Materials List

FINISHED DIMENSIONS

PARTS

A. Frame members (8) — ¾" x ¾" x 14¼"

B. Side slats (24) — ¼" x 2" x 10"

C. Bottom slats (5) — ¼" x 2" x 14¼"

D. Narrow bottom slat — ¼" x 1¾" x 14¼"

HARDWARE

¾" Wire brads (75-100)

EXPLODED VIEW

1

Adjust the size of the boxes to your needs.
As we designed the boxes, they are 14¼″ square and
10¼″ deep. At this size, they will hold most small and
medium-sized items. However, you may need boxes of
another size. If so, the dimensions can be adjusted easily
by simply making the slats and frame members longer or
shorter. If you make the boxes larger than 16″ square and
12″ deep, you will also have to increase the width and
the thickness of the various parts.

Use this chart to determine the dimensions:

Size of the Box	Frame Members	Slats
Up to 12″ x 16″ x 16″	¾″ x ¾″	¼″ x 2″
Up to 16″ x 20″ x 20″	1⅛″ x 1⅛″	⅜″ x 2″
Up to 20″ x 24″ x 24″	1½″ x 1½″	½″ x 2″

Don't make the boxes *too* big. You won't be able to carry
them comfortably when they're loaded.

2

Cut all parts to size.   After you've deter-
mined the size of your boxes, cut all the parts to
size. Since so many of the parts are the same size, use a
stop block on your table saw or radial arm saw to help
you quickly measure and cut parts to precisely the same
length. (See Figures 1 and 2.)

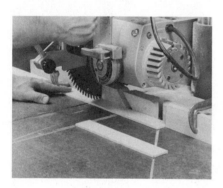

1/When using a stop
block on your radial
arm saw, attach the
block to the backstop.
If the length of the
parts you want to
duplicate is longer
than your backstop,
you may have to
make a new, longer
backstop.

2/When using a stop
block on your table
saw, attach the block
to a long, wooden
miter gauge "face."
You'll have to make
this piece. Most miter
gauges have holes or
slots so that you can
easily attach wooden
faces.

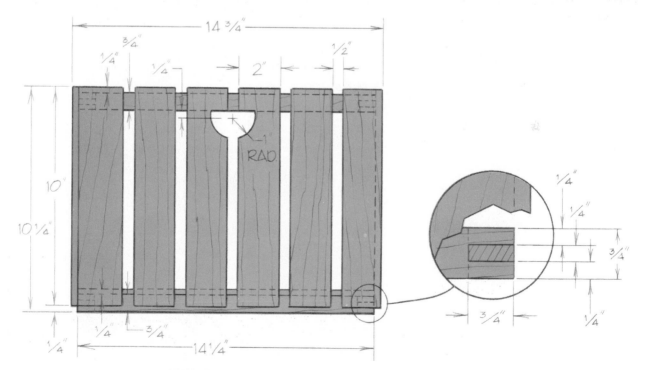

FRONT VIEW   **BRIDLE JOINT DETAIL**

3 Cut the bridle joints in the frame members.

The frame members are joined with open or "slot" mortises and tenons, commonly called "bridle joints." These joints are easy to make on your table saw, but they require a "tenoning jig." Some manufacturers of saws sell these jigs as accessories. But you can make your own with very little trouble from a few scraps of wood. As you can see in Figures 3 and 4, the jig is just a board, 8″ to 10″ wide, that rides along the fence. A narrow strip mounted near the back of this wide board helps to align the stock in the jig and keep it square to the saw blade as you cut the mortises and tenons.

To make a bridle joint, start with the mortises. First adjust the height of the saw blade above the table, using the width of the stock as a gauge. Clamp the stock in the jig and align the rip fence so that the blade will cut a ⅛″-wide kerf in the edge of the board, ¼″ in from the face. (This kerf forms *half* of the mortise.) Pass the stock over the blade, turn it around in the jig (edge for edge), and pass it over the blade again. (See Figure 3.) The completed mortise should be ¼″ wide, as shown in the *Bridle Joint Detail.* Cut mortises in *one* end of all the frame members.

Cut tenons in the other end of the members. Readjust the position of the rip fence so that the blade will cut the "cheeks" of the tenon. Once again, pass the stock over the blade, turn it around in the jig, and pass it over the blade a second time. (See Figure 4.) Repeat for all the frame members. To complete the tenons, set the jig aside. Readjust the height of the table saw to cut the "shoulders," and clamp a stop block to the rip fence to help gauge the length of the tenon. Using the miter gauge to guide the stock, pass it over the blade, turn it over (face for face), and pass it over the blade again. (See Figure 5.)

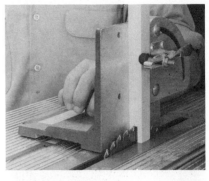

3/To make a bridle joint, first cut the mortise. Use a tenoning jig to hold the stock square to the blade.

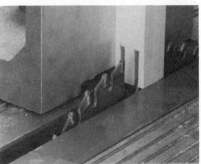

4/Next, cut the cheeks of the tenon. Once again, use a tenoning jig to hold the stock.

5/Complete the tenon by cutting the shoulders. Use a miter gauge to guide the stock, and a stop block to help gauge the length of the tenon. The stop block will ensure that both shoulders are even.

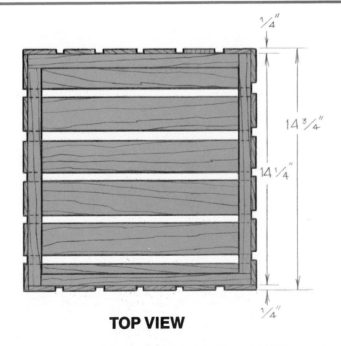

¼″

14 ¾″

14 ¼″

¼″

TOP VIEW

4 *Finish sand the parts.* Finish sand the frame members and slats. Be careful not to round over or "break" any edges where two boards will be joined.

If you plan to paint the boxes, you need not do a "finish" sanding. Just remove any splinters and defects in the surfaces of the boards.

5 *Assemble the boxes.* Join the frame members with glue, inserting the tenon of one member into the mortise of the next. Check that each frame is perfectly square before you clamp the bridle joints.

Let the frames sit for at least twenty-four hours, so the glue will cure completely. (Even though some glues advertise that they "set" in an hour or less, few glues can withstand the stress of hammering or machining until they are *completely* cured. This usually takes twenty-four hours.) Divide up the completed assemblies into bottom and top frames.

Glue the bottom slats to the bottom frames, tacking them in place with brads. (These brads don't add much strength to the joints; they simply keep the slats in place while the glue cures.) Once again, let the frames sit for twenty-four hours so the glue can dry completely.

Finally, join the bottom and top frames with the side slats. Glue and tack these slats in place, just as you did with the bottom slats. Attach the corner slats first, then "fill in" the rest of the slats between them. Note that the top frames are recessed ¼″ in from the ends of the slats, and the bottom frames protrude ¼″. This forms interlocking "lips," so that the boxes will lock themselves together when you stack them.

TRY THIS! Because the top frames are not reinforced with slats like the bottom frames, you'll probably find they "give" quite a bit when you try to hammer the brads. To prevent this, position each frame so that it straddles the corner of your workbench.

6 *Cut the handholds.* Mark the handholds on two opposing sides of the boxes, where shown in the *Front View.* Then cut out these handholds with a sabre saw.

7 *Apply a finish to the completed boxes.* Finish sand any parts of the boxes that may still need it. Then apply paint, stain, or a clear finish to the boxes, if you so desire. If you plan to use them in your garage, attic, or basement, you may not want to go to the trouble of finishing them. Just leave them "raw."

Closet Organizers

Consider how closets are usually built: There's a single rod running from side to side, about 66″ above the floor, and a shelf above that. Clothes, no matter what their length, hang on the rod. Shoes are piled on the floor, and everything else is stuffed on the shelf. The shelf is full; the floor is cluttered; but there's a lot of vacant space between the shoes and the hanging clothes.

By reorganizing your closet, you can turn that vacant space into *usable* storage space. We've created four simple storage modules to help you do this.

■ A *hanger shelf,* equipped with a rod beneath it, can be hung at any level you need.

■ An *adjustable trapeze* can be mounted on an existing rod (or on the rod under the hanger shelf) to create two levels on which to hang clothes.

■ A *vertical storage unit* has drawers and adjustable shelves to store linens, sweaters, socks — anything that is better stored on a shelf or in a drawer.

■ A *horizontal storage unit* also has shelves and drawers. It fits across the bottom of your closet, and, while it holds almost anything that can be stored in the vertical unit, it's particularly useful for storing shoes.

Install one — or several — of these modules inside your closet to help make better use of it. ✻

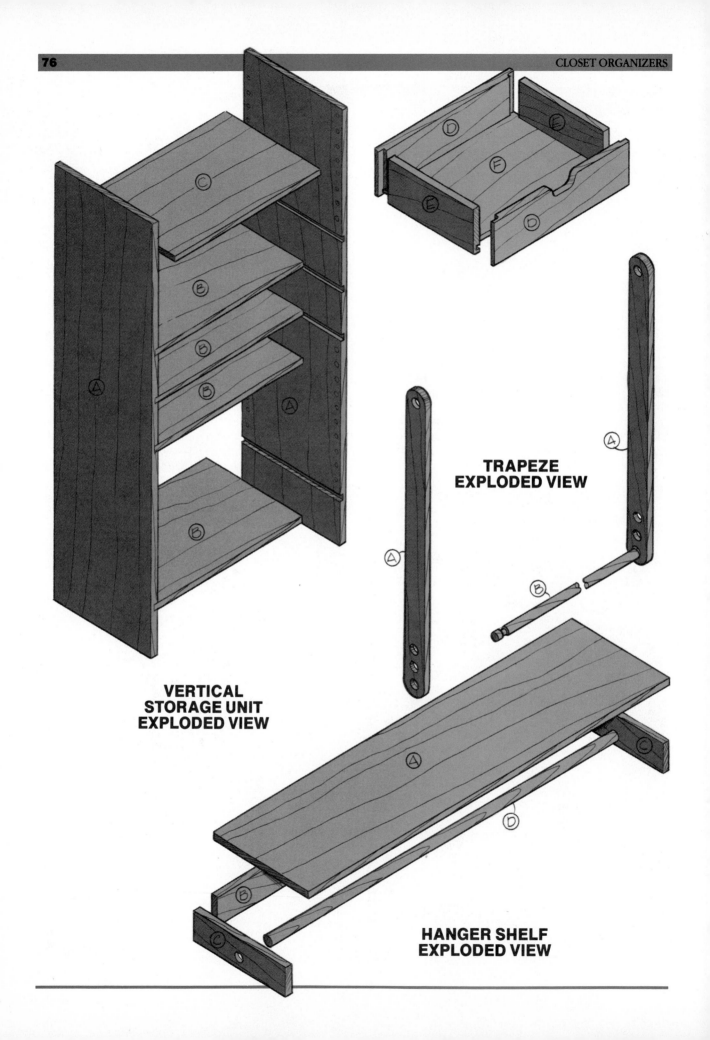

**TRAPEZE
EXPLODED VIEW**

**VERTICAL
STORAGE UNIT
EXPLODED VIEW**

**HANGER SHELF
EXPLODED VIEW**

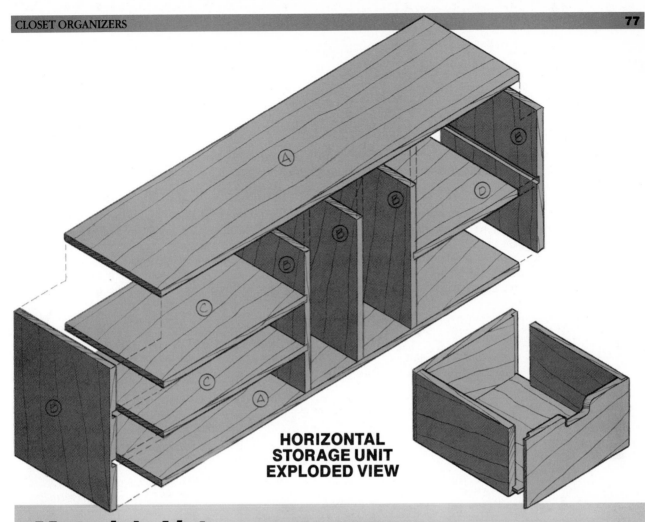

**HORIZONTAL
STORAGE UNIT
EXPLODED VIEW**

Materials List

FINISHED DIMENSIONS

PARTS

Hanger Shelf

A. Shelf   ¾" x 16" x (variable)

B. Backboard   ¾" x 4" x (variable)

C. Ends (2)   ¾" x 4" x 16"

D. Rod   1¼" dia. x (variable)

Vertical Storage Unit

A. Sides   ¾" x 16" x (variable)

B. Fixed
shelves (2-4)   ¾" x 16" x (variable)

C. Adjustable
shelves (1-4)   ¾" x 16" x (variable)

D. Drawer front/
back (4)   ¾" x 5¹⁵/₁₆" x (variable)

E. Drawer
sides (4)   ¾" x 5¹⁵/₁₆" x 15¼"

F. Drawer
bottoms (2)   ¼" x 15" x (variable)

Trapeze

A. Supports (2)   ¾" x 3" x 42"

B. Rod   1¼" dia. x (variable)

Horizontal Storage Unit

A. Top/
bottom (2)   ¾" x 16" x (variable)

B. Sides/
dividers (3-5)   ¾" x 16" x 19½"

C. Shelves (2-3) ¾" x 16" x (variable)

D. Drawer
support   ¾" x 16" x (variable)

E. Drawer front/
back (4)   ¾" x 9⁵/₁₆" x (variable)

F. Drawer
sides (4)   ¾" x 9⁵/₁₆" x 15¼"

G. Drawer
bottoms (2)   ¼" x 15" x (variable)

HARDWARE

Hanger Shelf

#10 x 1¼" Flathead wood screws
(8-10)

Trapeze

(No hardware required.)

Vertical Storage Unit

#10 x 1¼" Flathead wood screws
(24-36)

4d Finishing nails (¼ lb.)

Pin-type shelving supports (12-24)

Horizontal Storage Unit

#10 x 1¼" Flathead wood screws
(24-36)

4d Finishing nails (¼ lb.)

Planning the Project

1 ***Decide how you want to rearrange your closet.*** Before you can build any of the modules, you need to plan which ones you will use and how you will install them in the closet. Carefully measure the interior of your closet and the size of its opening so you know how much room you have to work with.

Next, list what you want to store in the closet. What sorts of clothes do you have? How many hanging items, how many folding items, how many shoes, hats, belts, ties, and accessories? Is the closet just for clothes? Or do you have other items — toys, sports equipment, bed linens, and so on? Make a general inventory and list which items would be best stored in or on what modules. This will indicate which modules you need to build.

Finally, draw a rough plan of how the modules will be arranged in the closet. We show three possibilities here, for a man, woman, and young child. You may choose an arrangement similar to one of these — or you may come up with something very different. In any case, it is important that the arrangement serve your needs.

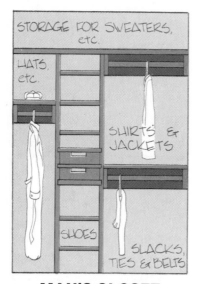

MAN'S CLOSET

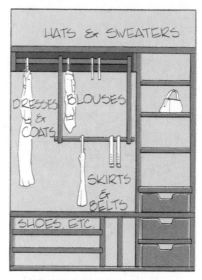

WOMAN'S CLOSET

CHILD'S CLOSET

2 ***Figure the dimensions of the modules and the parts.*** Once you have a plan that you're comfortable with, calculate the sizes of the modules you need to build. From this, figure the dimensions of all the various parts, and fill in the measurements marked "variable" in the Materials List. You may also want to change some measurements that *aren't* marked "variable," such as the size of the drawer parts or the width of the shelves. All the measurements in the list are just suggestions; they can all be changed to suit you.

Note: We show most of the modules (except for the trapeze) 16″ deep. This dimension will fit most closets and allows you ample room to hang clothes on an ordinary hanger. (Hangers are 15″-16″ wide.) The hanger shelf should not be made any narrower than this.

3 ***Determine the materials that you need.*** Once you have figured all the measurements, add up the sizes of the parts and determine the amount of lumber you need. You will probably make the modules from plywood, since most of the parts are wider than ordinary dimension lumber. If this is the case, purchase cabinet-grade plywood and veneer tape to cover exposed plies.

Making the Hanger Shelf

1 ***Cut the parts to size.*** Double-check your measurements, then cut the parts to the sizes that you have figured. Make the rod from 1¼″-diameter closet pole. This is available at most lumberyards.

2 ***Drill the holes for the rods.*** The hanger shelf module is assembled entirely with butt joints, and the only "joinery" is the 1¼″-diameter holes in the ends that hold the rod. Make these holes with a hole saw. To prevent tear-out, saw the hole halfway through the stock from one side, then turn the stock over and complete the hole. The pilot (the drill bit in the center of the hole saw) will position the saw precisely when you turn the board over.

3 ***Sand the parts.*** Sand or scrape all the parts smooth, removing any saw marks. Be careful not to round over or "break" any corners or edges that will abut other parts.

4 ***Assemble the hanger shelf.*** Dry assemble all the parts to test their fit. When you're satisfied they fit properly, assemble the parts with glue and screws. Do *not* attach the rod permanently in its holes. Leave it loose so that you can remove it to install a trapeze, if you so desire.

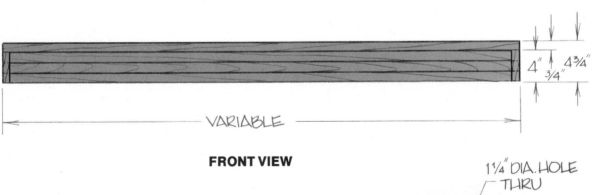

FRONT VIEW

HANGER SHELF

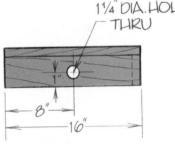

SIDE VIEW

Making the Trapeze

1 **Cut the parts to size.** Double-check your measurements, then cut the parts to the sizes that you have figured. As you did with the hanger shelf, make the rod from closet pole.

2 **Drill the holes in the supports.** If you're hanging this trapeze on an existing rod in your closet, measure the diameter of the rod. Drill the holes in the supports 1/16″–1/8″ larger than the rod. Thus, if it will hang from 1¼″-diameter closet pole, under a hanger shelf, drill 1⅜″-diameter holes, as shown in the *Trapeze/Side View*. Make these holes with a hole saw.

3 **Round the ends of the supports.** The ends of the rods are rounded to prevent them from catching on your clothes. Cut this shape with a band saw or sabre saw.

4 **Cut grooves near the ends of the rod.** The adjustable rod that mounts in the trapeze must have two grooves in it, one groove near each end. These keep the rod from sliding out of the holes in the supports. To make the groove, mount the rod on your lathe and cut it with a flat chisel.

If you don't have a lathe, carefully score the rod with a back saw to mark the sides of each groove. (See Figure 1.) Then remove the waste with a *very* sharp chisel. (See Figure 2.) After you've chiseled away most of the waste, remove the last little bit with a file or rasp.

1/To cut a kerf just ¼″ deep, clamp two scraps of wood on either side of your back saw, ¼″ above the teeth. These will serve as stop blocks.

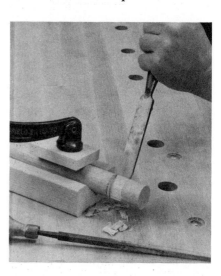

2/Place the rod in a V-jig after you cut the kerfs that mark both sides of the grooves. This will help to hold the rod steady while you chisel the waste out from between the kerfs.

5 **Sand and assemble the parts.** Sand or scrape all the parts smooth, removing any saw marks. Assemble the three parts when you install the trapeze in your closet.

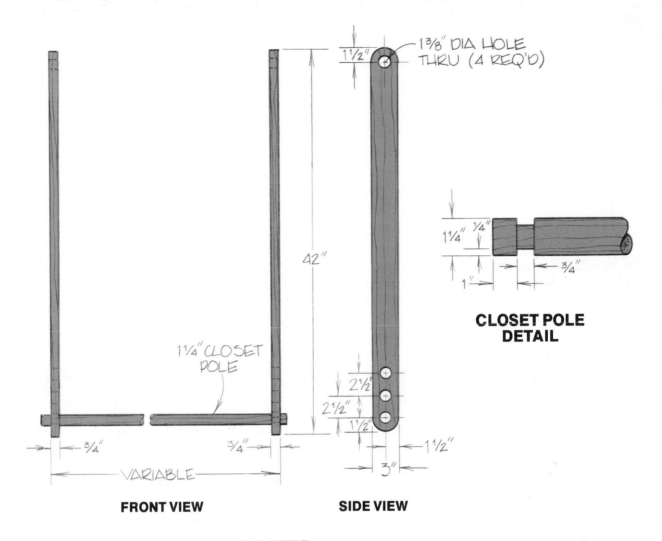

1 3/8" DIA HOLE THRU (4 REQ'D)

CLOSET POLE DETAIL

FRONT VIEW

SIDE VIEW

TRAPEZE

Making the Vertical and Horizontal Storage Units

The cutting, machining, and assembly of the vertical and horizontal storage units are exactly the same — both have similar joinery and components. The following instructions will serve for both:

1 *Cut the parts to size.* As you have done before, double-check your measurements. Then cut the parts to the sizes that you have calculated. Make the adjustable shelves and the drawer fronts/backs 1/8" narrower than the space between the sides so they won't bind.

2

Make the joinery. All of the dadoes, rabbets and grooves in the various parts of these storage units can be made with a router and straight bits, or a dado cutter. Start with the narrower joints and work your way up to the wider ones — or work the other way around. To help keep track, here's a list of the joints:

■ ¼"-wide x ¼"-deep grooves near the bottom inside edge of the drawer fronts, backs, and sides, to hold the bottoms

■ ¾"-wide x ⅜"-deep dadoes in the sides and dividers to hold the fixed shelves and drawer supports

■ ¾"-wide x ½"-deep rabbets in the drawer fronts and backs, to attach the sides

If you're making adjustable shelves, drill ¼"-diameter, ⅜"-deep stopped holes in the sides, as shown in the *Side Layout.*

3

Cut the drawer hand-holds. The drawer "pulls" are simple notches in the drawer fronts, as shown in the *Vertical Storage Unit/Front View* and *Horizontal Storage Unit/Front View.* Cut these notches with a band saw or sabre saw.

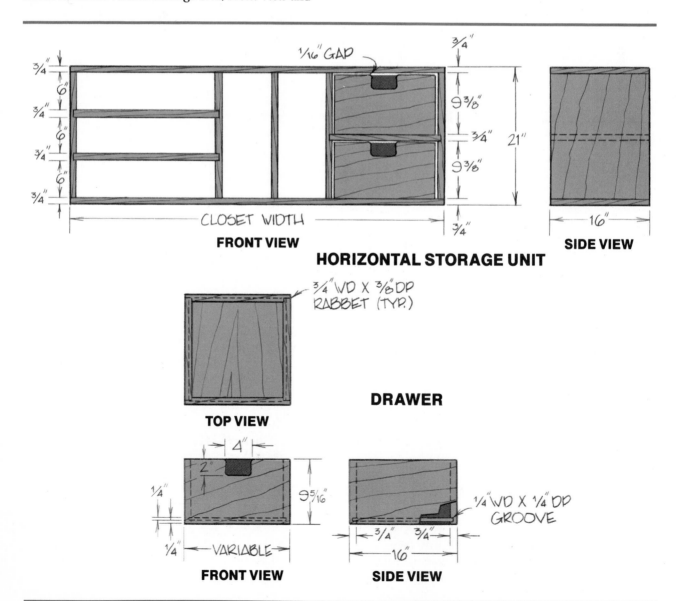

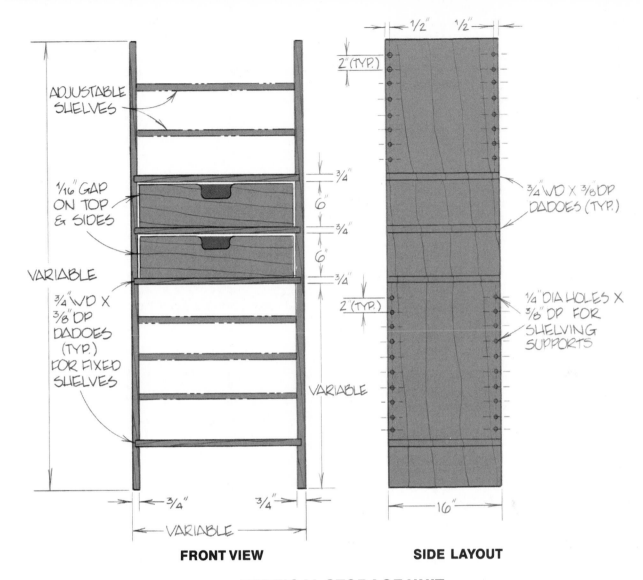

ADJUSTABLE SHELVES

¹/₁₆" GAP ON TOP & SIDES

VARIABLE

¾" WD X ⅜" DP DADOES (TYP.) FOR FIXED SHELVES

3/4"

6"

3/4"

6"

3/4"

VARIABLE

¾" 3/4"

VARIABLE

FRONT VIEW

½" ½"

2" (TYP.)

¾" WD X ⅜" DP DADOES (TYP.)

2" (TYP.)

¼" DIA HOLES X ⅜" DP FOR SHELVING SUPPORTS

16"

SIDE LAYOUT

VERTICAL STORAGE UNIT

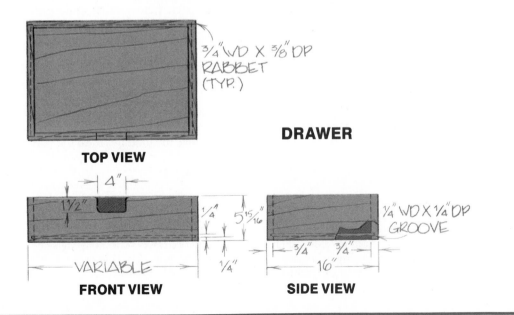

¾" WD X ⅜" DP RABBET (TYP.)

TOP VIEW

DRAWER

4"

1½"

¼"

5¹⁵/₁₆"

VARIABLE

¼"

FRONT VIEW

¼" WD X ¼" DP GROOVE

¾" ¾"

16"

SIDE VIEW

4 **Sand the parts.** Sand or scrape all the parts smooth, removing any saw marks. Pay special attention to the notches in the drawer fronts. Round the edges of these notches to make them comfortable to grab — and to decrease the possibility of splinters. Be careful not to round over any corners or edges that abut other parts.

5 **Assemble the case.** Dry assemble the sides, dividers (if any) and fixed shelves to test the fit. When you're satisfied that all the parts fit properly, reassemble them with glue and screws. As you clamp the parts together, ensure that the case is square.

6 **Assemble the drawers.** As you did with the case, dry assemble the drawers to test the fit of the parts. Also test the fit of the drawers in the case. When you're satisfied with both, reassemble the drawer with glue and finishing nails. Drive the finishing nails through the side and into the rabbeted ends of the drawer fronts and backs. "Set" the heads of the nails below the surface of the wood, and cover them with wood putty. *Do not* glue or nail the bottoms in the drawers; let them "float" in the grooves.

TRY THIS! To help the drawers slide smoothly in and out of the case, apply paraffin to the bottom edges.

Installing the Modules

1 **Remove the existing rods and shelves from your closet.** After you have finished all the modules and they are ready to install, take the clothes (or whatever you have stored) from your closet and pack them away temporarily. Then remove the existing rods and shelves.

2 **Test fit the modules in the closet.** Temporarily place the modules in the closet to ensure they fit correctly. If they're too tight, you may have to plane some surfaces. If they're too loose, you will have to make shims. When you're satisfied with how they fit, remove the modules from the closet.

3 **Finish the modules.** If you have used plywood to make these modules, cover all the visible edges with veneer tape. Do any necessary touch-up sanding, and apply a stain, paint, or other finish to the modules. Finish only the fronts of the drawers. The interiors of drawers should always be left "raw" so they absorb moisture. This, in turn, prevents your clothes from smelling musty.

4 ***Install the modules.*** Working from the floor up, permanently install the modules in the closet. Attach the horizontal units to the floor with wood screws, and to the back wall with metal brackets or cleats. Also use brackets and cleats to attach the vertical units to the back wall. If one side of a storage unit butts up against a side wall, secure the unit to the wall studs with wood screws. Hang the trapezes from the hanger shelves *before* you install the shelves. Attach the hanger shelves to the walls of the closet by driving wood screws through the backboard and the ends and into the wall studs. Do *not* use glue, just in case you need to remove the modules — or rearrange the closet — at some later date.

Drill Press Worktable

A drill press is essential for woodworking operations in which you must bore holes at precise angles or to precise depths. Most drill presses, unfortunately, come with small tables that are better suited for metalworking than woodworking. To perform even some common woodworking operations, you may need to fit your machine with a special woodworking worktable.

This worktable has several important features. First, the surface is large, so the work will be better supported. It tilts *front-to-back,* enabling you to drill angled holes in long pieces. It has an adjustable fence, which helps to both guide and hold the work. You can also attach jigs and fixtures to this fence. Finally, there is a slot for a miter gauge. This, too, helps to hold and guide the work.

You can easily make this worktable in your shop. Use plywood or laminate-covered particleboard, which won't warp, for the table and the base. Make the trunnions and other parts from clear, straight hardwood. Cut the curved grooves in the trunnions with a sabre saw and the miter gauge slot with a router or dado cutter. Assemble the parts of the worktable with wood screws and carriage bolts, then attach it to your drill press table with large screws or bolts.

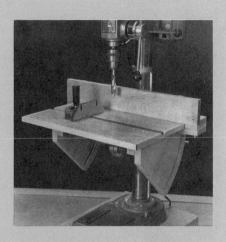

This special worktable enables you to perform many special woodworking operations on your drill press. It attaches to your existing drill press table.

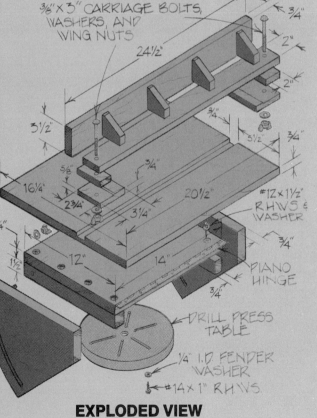

TRUNNION LAYOUT

EXPLODED VIEW

Super-Quick Shelves

If yours is like most homes, it seems you never have enough shelving space. The minute you build a set of shelves, presto! — they're loaded to capacity. In a few months (or, sometimes, just a few days), you need another set of shelves.

These units can help to reduce much of the time and the money it takes you to solve your shelving crisis. The joinery and the construction have been simplified as much as possible without sacrificing strength or durability. You can actually build these shelves from scratch *faster* than you can put together most store-bought shelving kits. Depending on the materials that you use, you will probably be able to put them together a good deal cheaper, too.

Furthermore, the same basic design can be used to make both utility and formal shelving units. To create a set of utility shelves, simply assemble the units so that the shelves are supported between four L-shaped uprights, one at each corner. To give your shelves a more finished look, add the optional trim at the top and bottom. ✷

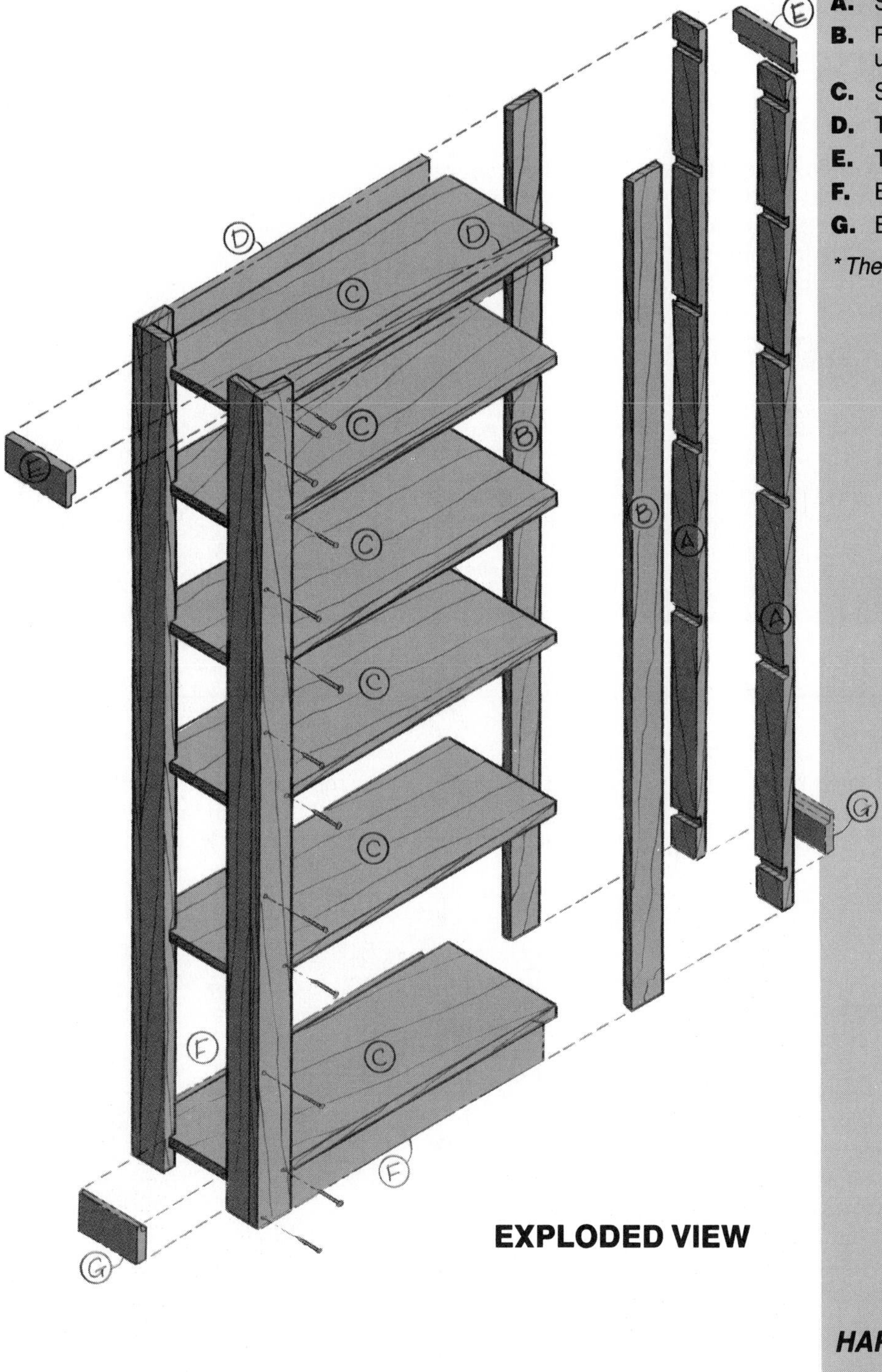

Materials List

FINISHED DIMENSIONS

PARTS

A. Side uprights (4)   ¾" x 2½" x 72"

B. Front/back
uprights (4)   ¾" x 3" x 72"

C. Shelves (6)   ¾" x 11" x 31¼"

D. Top long trim* (4)   ¾" x 2¾" x 26"

E. Top short trim* (4)   ¾" x 2¾" x 6"

F. Bottom long trim* (2)   ¾" x 3" x 26"

G. Bottom short trim* (2)   ¾" x 3" x 6"

* These parts are optional.

EXPLODED VIEW

HARDWARE

6d Finishing nails (¼ lb.)

1 **Cut the pieces to size.** To make one shelving unit, you'll need approximately 32 board feet of lumber, surfaced to ¾″ thick. If you're building this project to use as utility shelves, purchase inexpensive #2 pine "dimension" lumber. You'll need 3 pieces 1 x 12 x 6′ and 2 pieces 1 x 12 x 8′ per unit.

Once you have gathered the lumber, cut the parts to the sizes shown on the Materials List. If you're using dimension lumber, make the uprights and the optional trim from the 6′-long pieces and the shelves from the 8′-long pieces. *Do not* rip the side uprights to their final width just yet. Wait until *after* you have cut the dadoes.

2 **Make the joinery in the side uprights.** In this project, the shelves are held in place by dadoes in the side uprights. You can save some time by cutting these dadoes in a wide board, then ripping the uprights from that board. Select stock at least 10⅜″

wide, and rout or saw the dadoes where shown on the *Side Uprights Cutting Diagram.* Then rip this board into 2½″-wide strips to make four uprights. (See Figures 1 and 2.)

1/To make the side uprights, first make dadoes in a wide board. If you're using a router to cut these joints, a large T-square made from scrap wood will help you to quickly position the dadoes and guide the router.

2/The side upright stock must be at least 10⅜″ wide so that you can rip four 2½″-wide strips from it. If you plan to joint the edges of the uprights, or if the kerf of your saw blade is more than ⅛″, the stock should be slightly wider.

3 **Make the joinery in the side trim (optional).** If you have elected to add the optional trim to this project, cut a ¾″-wide, ⅜″-deep

rabbet in one edge of the top and bottom *short* trim parts. You can make these rabbets with the same setup you used to make the dadoes in the side uprights.

4 **Assemble the front, back, and side frames (optional).** If you're adding the optional trim, you must assemble four "frames," using the uprights as stiles and the trim as rails. Join these parts with dowels, splines, or "biscuits." When assembling the side frames, make certain that the rabbets in the short trim pieces line up with the top and bottom dadoes in the side uprights. (See Figure 3.) As you clamp the frames, check that the assemblies are square.

3/To ensure that the dadoes in the uprights and the rabbets in the trim line up properly, cut a ¾″-thick scrap of wood and clamp it in these joints while the glue on the frame assembly is curing. To keep glue from sticking to the scrap, cover it in plastic wrap.

5 **Finish sand all parts and assemblies (optional).** If you are making a set of formal shelves, sand and smooth the shelves and frame assem-

blies. Be careful not to round over any edges or corners that join to other parts. If you're making a set of utility shelves, you may skip the sanding.

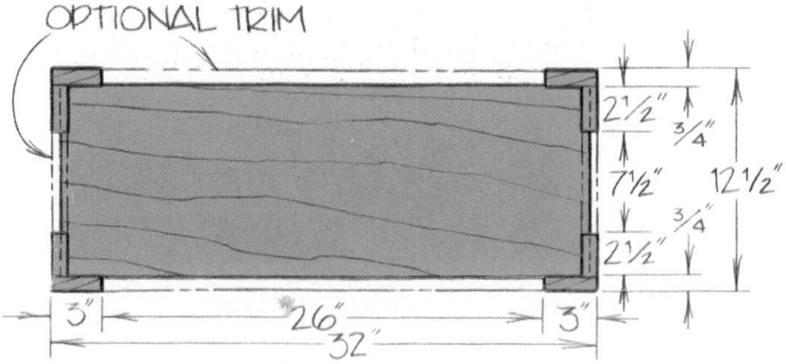
OPTIONAL TRIM
2½"
¾"
7½"
12½"
¾"
2½"
3"
26"
3"
32"

TOP VIEW

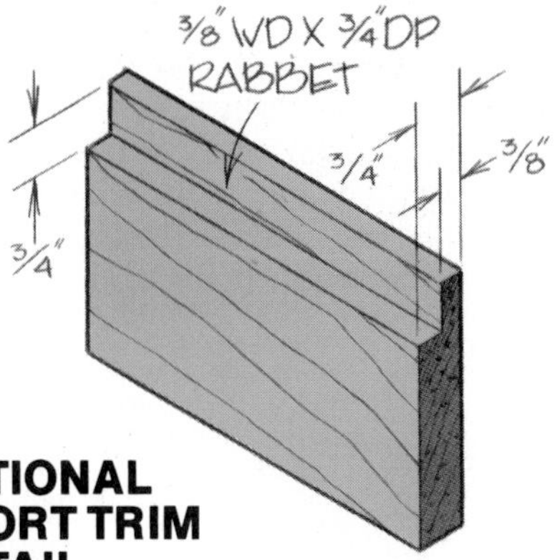
⅜" WD X ¾" DP RABBET
¾"
⅜"
¾"

OPTIONAL SHORT TRIM DETAIL

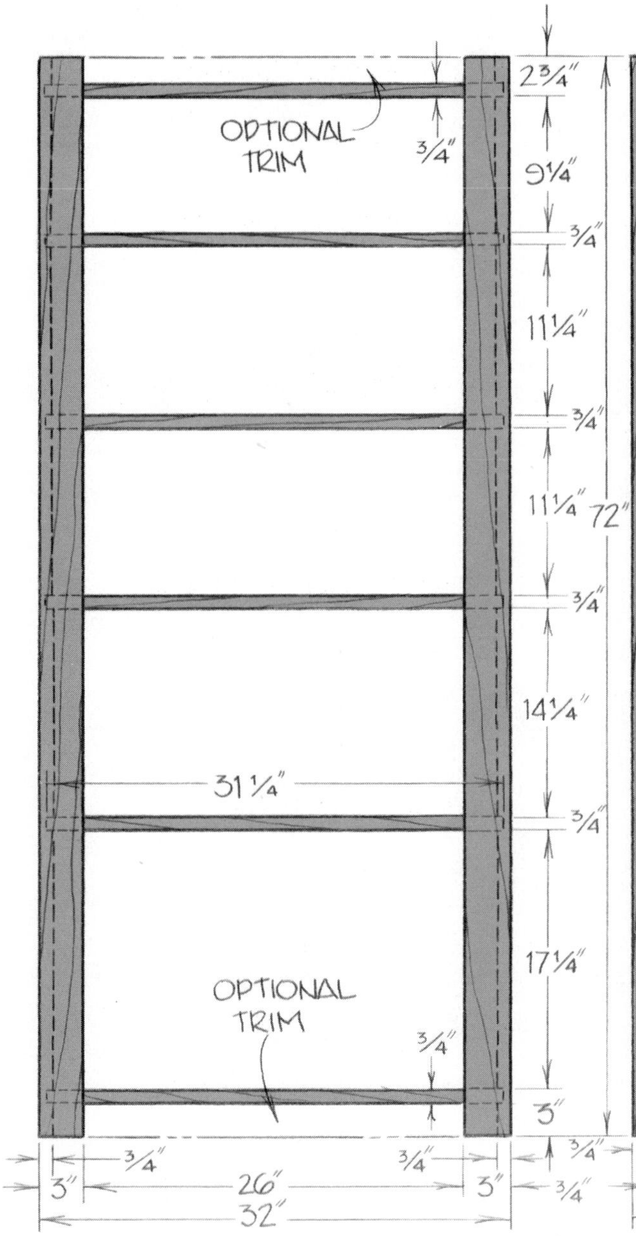
OPTIONAL TRIM
¾"
2¾"
9¼"
¾"
11¼"
¾"
11¼"
72"
¾"
14¼"
31¼"
¾"
17¼"
OPTIONAL TRIM
¾"
3"
¾"
¾"
¾"
3"
26"
3"
¾"
32"

FRONT VIEW

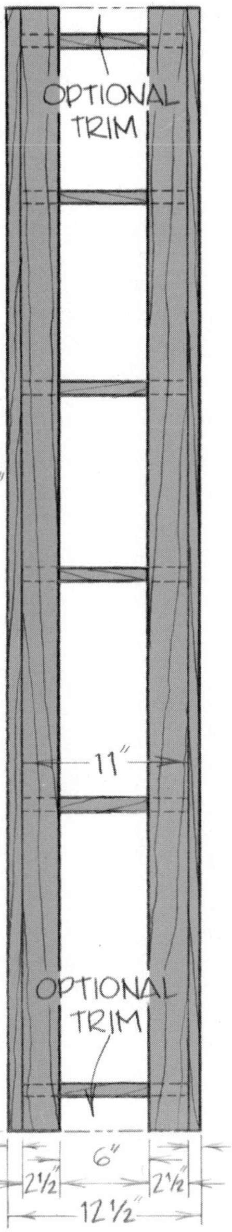
OPTIONAL TRIM
11"
OPTIONAL TRIM
6"
2½"
2½"
12½"

SIDE VIEW

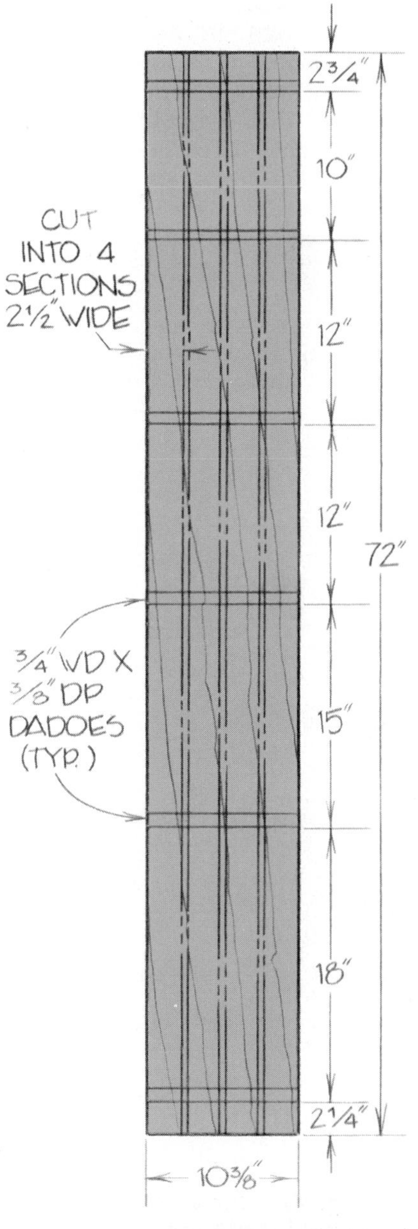
CUT INTO 4 SECTIONS 2½" WIDE
¾" WD X ⅜" DP DADOES (TYP.)
2¾"
10"
12"
12"
72"
15"
18"
2¼"
10⅜"

SIDE UPRIGHTS CUTTING DIAGRAM

6

Assemble the shelves and the side uprights (or frames). Spread glue in the dadoes and the rabbets of the side uprights or frames. Fasten the uprights/frames to the ends of the shelving with 6d finishing nails. Using a punch, set each nail slightly below the surface of the wood.

TRY THIS! When nailing up large assemblies, don't hammer the nails home until you've finished the assembly. Let the heads protrude until you're sure that all the parts are properly positioned. That way, if you have to reposition a part, you can easily remove the nails that hold it.

7

Join the front and back uprights (or frames) to the shelving assembly. Fit the front and back uprights/frames to the shelving assembly. Mark the edges of the shelves where the uprights/frames join to them. Remove the uprights/frames, and spread glue on just those surfaces of the shelving assembly where the front/back uprights/frames will join. Be careful not to apply any glue past the marks that you've made on the shelves.

Fasten the front and back uprights/frames to the shelving assembly with 6d nails. As you did before with the side uprights/frames, set the head of each nail slightly below the surface of the wood.

TRY THIS! In some instances, you may want to add the optional trim *after* you assemble the shelving unit. Perhaps you wish to transform a set of existing utility shelves into something more formal. Or maybe you want to save the time it takes to join the uprights and trim to make the frames. In either case, there is a simple way to attach the trim to the assembled shelves.

First, *fit* the trim parts to the assembly. You may have to cut them slightly longer or shorter than indicated in the Materials List, depending on how the shelving unit may have expanded or shrunk since you built it. Then attach the trim to the edges of the top and bottom shelves with nails and glue.

Finally, attach the trim to the uprights with small blocks of wood or gussets. Nail and glue these gussets to the *back* side of the trim and the uprights (where they won't be seen), so that the gussets straddle the joints between the two parts. The grain of the gussets should be parallel to the trim so that it bridges the joint.

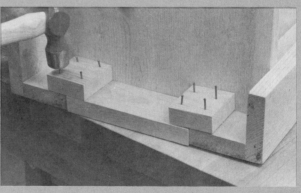

8

Apply a finish to the completed shelves (optional). Using a plane, true the corners where the side uprights/frames join the front and back uprights/frames. Cover the nail heads with wood putty.

Do any necessary touch-up sanding, and apply a finish to the completed project. Of course, if you're making a set of utility shelves, you may not need to finish the shelves.

Slide-Out Bins and Shelves

Your kitchen and bathroom cabinets are among the most useful, most essential storage units in your home. Think of all the things you store in them!

But the space inside these cabinets is not always perfectly suited to the items you have to store. Consider all your pots and pans, each with a lid. Retrieving a single pan from the middle of a stack near the back of a cabinet can be quite a chore. Take several pots or pans out of a cabinet to cook a meal, and the stacks quickly become a hopeless jumble. Or think how you strain to lift a mixer from the cabinet.

Slide-out bins and shelves help to make cabinet space more accessible and easier to organize. You create a "filing system" for the things that you want to store. When you want to retrieve an item, just open the cabinet doors and pull out the appropriate shelf or bin. Even those items at the back of the cabinet are within easy reach.

The bin and shelf shown here can be easily installed in your existing cabinets. They are assembled with ordinary rabbets, dadoes, and grooves. This simple joinery makes them quick to build. Moreover, the bin and the shelf are mounted on two wooden "runners." There is no expensive, complex hardware to install or adjust. You don't need to purchase special extension slides or pull-outs. In just a few evenings, you can outfit all of your cabinets with slide-out bins and shelves to make better use of the storage space inside your kitchen and bathroom cabinets. ●

Materials List

FINISHED DIMENSIONS

PARTS

A. Bin front/
     back (2)   ¾" x 10¾" x (variable)
B. Bin sides (2)   ¾" x 10¾" x (variable)
C. Bin
     bottom   ¼" x (variable) x (variable)
D. Bin dividers
     (2-4)   ¼" x 10¼" x (variable)
E. Shelf   ¾" x (variable) x (variable)
F. Shelf front/
     back trim (2)   ¾" x 1" x (variable)
G. Shelf side
     trim (2)   ¾" x 1" x (variable)
H. Backstop   ¾" x ¾" x (variable)
J. Runners (2)   ¾" x 3½" x (variable)
K. Runner
     supports (4)   ¾" x 1⅜" x 13"

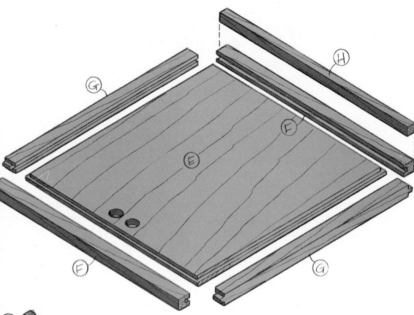

SHELF
EXPLODED VIEW

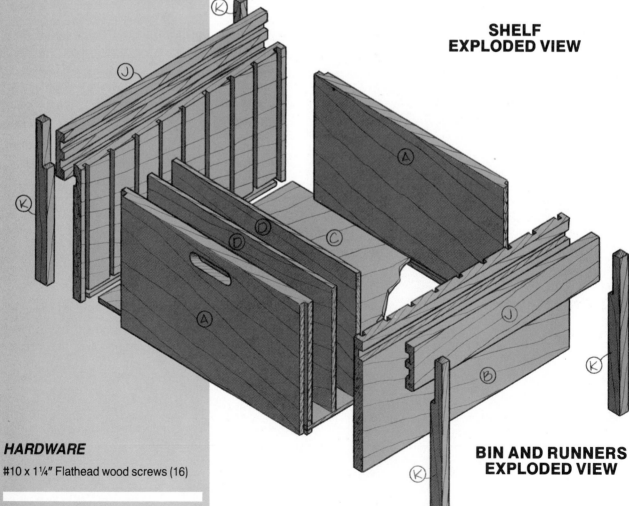

HARDWARE

#10 x 1¼" Flathead wood screws (16)

BIN AND RUNNERS
EXPLODED VIEW

1

Determine the size of the bin, shelf, and runners that you need. Carefully measure the inside of your cabinet. Determine the height and width of the opening and the depth of the cabinet, as well as the width of the stiles (vertical members) of the cabinet's face frame. Also determine the style of door on the cabinet. Is it flush, lipped, or overlapped? (See Figure 1.)

From this information, calculate the dimensions of the bin, shelf, and runners. When you figure the depth — the front-to-back dimension — remember that the front of the bin and the shelf must clear the backs of the door frame so that the door can close properly. When you figure the width, remember to leave a small gap between the bins or shelves and the face frame.

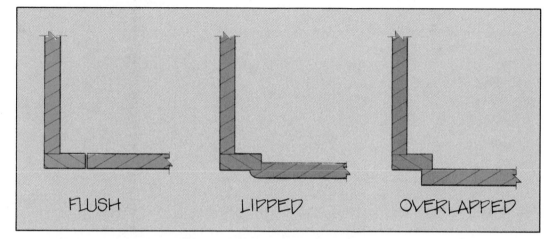

1/Here are the three basic types of cabinet doors: (1) flush, (2) lipped, and (3) overlapped. The bin and the shelf should clear the back of the cabinet door by at least ¼".

FLUSH   LIPPED   OVERLAPPED

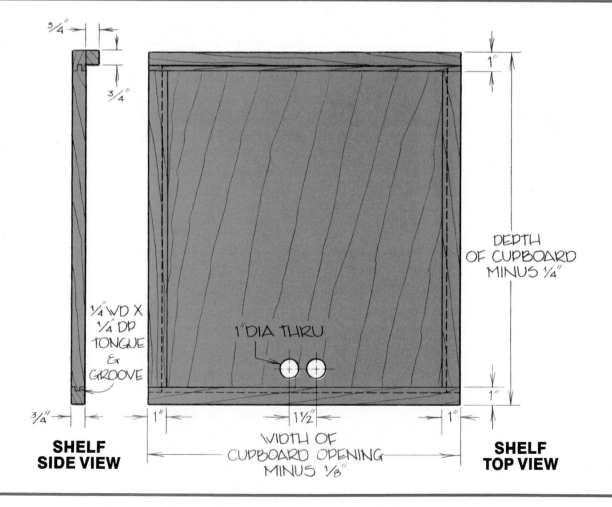

¾"

¾"

¼"WD X ¼" DP TONGUE & GROOVE

1"DIA THRU

DEPTH OF CUPBOARD MINUS ¼"

1"

1"

¾"   1"   1½"   1"

SHELF SIDE VIEW

WIDTH OF CUPBOARD OPENING MINUS ⅛"

SHELF TOP VIEW

2 ***Cut all parts to size.*** Once you have decided on the sizes of the bin, shelf and runners that you need, figure the sizes of the various parts, completing those measurements marked "variable" on the Materials List. Double-check your figures, then cut all the parts to the sizes you need.

> TRY THIS! Cut the shelf from a scrap of plywood. The trim will cover the plies, and the shelf will not change shape appreciably. A shelf made from solid wood will shrink and swell with changes in the weather and may eventually cup or warp.

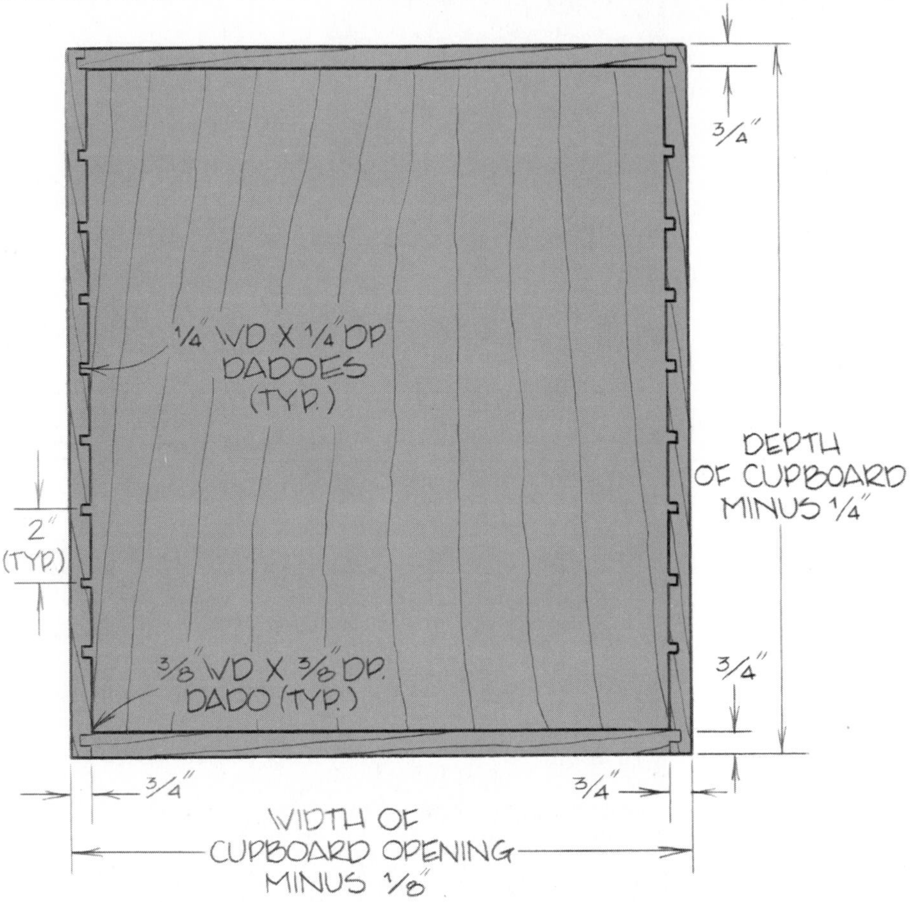
3/4"
1/4" WD X 1/4" DP DADOES (TYP.)
DEPTH OF CUPBOARD MINUS 1/4"
2" (TYP.)
3/8" WD X 3/8" DP. DADO (TYP.)
3/4"
3/4"
3/4"
WIDTH OF CUPBOARD OPENING MINUS 1/8"

BIN TOP VIEW

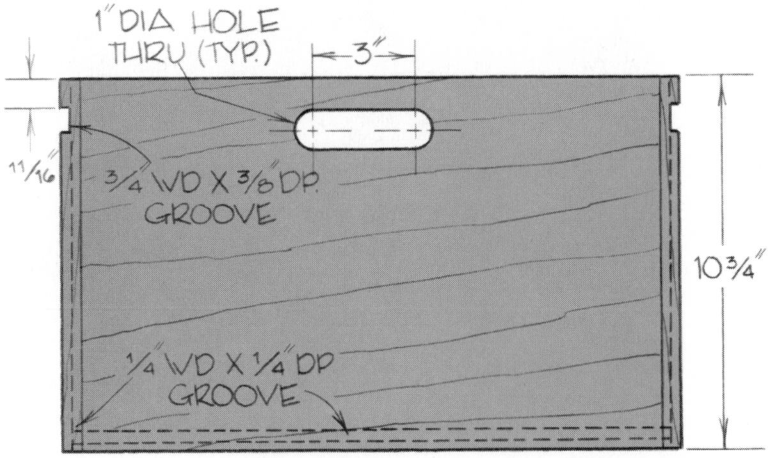
1" DIA HOLE THRU (TYP.)
3"
11/16"
3/4" WD X 3/8" DP. GROOVE
10 3/4"
1/4" WD X 1/4" DP GROOVE

BIN FRONT VIEW

3

Cut the joinery in the bin and shelf parts and the runners. All the dadoes, rabbets, and grooves in the various parts of this project can be cut with a router or a dado cutter. Start with the narrower joints and work your way up to the wider ones. Here's a list:

- ¼″-wide x ¼″-deep grooves in the bin front, back, and sides, to hold the bottom
- ¼″-wide x ¼″-deep dadoes in the bin sides to hold the dividers
- ¼″-wide x ¼″-deep grooves in the inside edge of the shelf trim to attach the trim to the shelf
- ¼″-wide x ¼″-thick tongues all around the edge of the shelf to attach the trim

    Make these tongues by cutting two rabbets, one in the bottom and one in the top face of the shelf. Also, cut tongues in the ends of the side trim. (See Figure 2.)
- ⅜″-wide x ⅜″-deep dadoes near the ends of the bin sides to attach the front and the back
- ⅜″-wide x ⅜″-deep rabbets in the ends of the bin front and back to attach the sides

- ¾″-wide x ⅜″-deep grooves near the top outside edge of the bin sides to hang the bins from the runners
- ¾″-wide x ⅜″-deep grooves in the runners to create guides for the bin
- ¹³/₁₆″-wide x ⅜″-deep grooves in the runners to create guides for the shelf

2/When you cut the tongue in the shelf side trim, use scrap to back up the stock. This will keep the slender trim parts from splintering.

4

Cut the notches in the runner supports. With a band saw or a hand saw, cut ⅜″-wide, 3½″-long notches in the runner supports. These notches will hold the runner at the proper height in the cabinet.

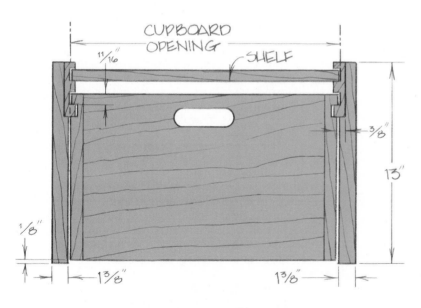

**BIN/SHELF/RUNNERS
FRONT VIEW**

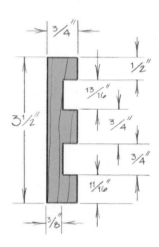

**RUNNER
DETAIL**

5

Cut the finger holes in the bin front and the shelf. Drill two 1″-diameter holes in the bin front, where shown in the *Bin/Front View.* Also, drill two 1″-diameter holes in the shelf, where shown in the *Shelf/Top View.* Using a sabre saw, remove the waste between the two holes in the bin front. You can also remove the waste between the holes in the shelf if you want, but it's not necessary. The shelf is normally a lot lighter than the bin, even when loaded down. All you need are two fingers to open it. The bin is heavier, and you will probably want to grip it with your entire hand.

6

Smooth all the parts. Sand or scrape all the parts, removing any saw marks or defects. Be careful not to round edges or corners that join other parts. Stop when the parts are smooth. There's no need to polish or "finish" sand these pieces, since they won't show when the cabinet doors are closed.

7

Assemble the bin and the shelf. Dry assemble the parts of the bin and the shelf to check their fit. When you're satisfied that all the pieces fit properly, reassemble them with glue. *Don't* glue the bottom in the bin; let it float free in the grooves. Also, don't glue the dividers in place in the bin. Leave these free so that you can rearrange them as the need arises.

8

Mount the runners in the cabinet. Dry assemble the runners and the runner supports inside the cabinet to make sure these parts will fit properly. The inside edges of the front runner supports must fit flush to the edges of the cabinet opening, and the runners must be parallel. When you're certain that the parts fit, fasten the runners to the runner supports with glue and #10 x 1¼″ flathead wood screws. Then mount the runner assemblies in the cabinet, attaching the supports to the cabinet backs and the face frame with screws. (See Figure 3.)

TRY THIS! Positioning the runners may involve some adjusting, so "tack" the runner assemblies in the cabinet with finishing nails at first. Don't drive the nails all the way home; leave the heads sticking out so that you can remove them easily. After you have nailed the runner assemblies in place, slide the bin and the shelf onto the runners and check the action. If the runners need to be repositioned, pull out the nails and tack them down in a new place. When you get the runners where you want them, remove the nails one at a time and replace them with wood screws.

This method of mounting the runners won't work for all cabinets, and you may have to improvise a mounting system for your particular cabinet design. Two common variations in cabinet construction, different from the cabinet we show here, are cabinets without face frames and cabinets with double-wide door openings. In both cases, the mounting system for the runners will have to be modified.

If the cabinet does not have a face frame, or the stiles of the face frame are too narrow, then there will be nothing to which you can attach the front runner supports. Instead, discard the supports and attach the runners directly to the sides of the cabinet with wood screws. You'll have to make the bin and the shelf slightly

3/Attach the runner assemblies inside the cabinets with screws. Do not glue them in place, in case you ever want to remove the bin and shelf.

smaller than you would if there were a face frame, but you won't lose a lot of storage space.

If the cabinet has a double-wide opening, with two doors and no middle stiles, you'll probably want to make two bins and two shelves to fit the opening. An extra-wide bin and shelf would be too heavy and too awkward. To mount the runners in the middle of the opening, attach a vertical member — a hidden stile — near the front of the cabinet, using cleats and screws. Notch this vertical member to hold the runners.

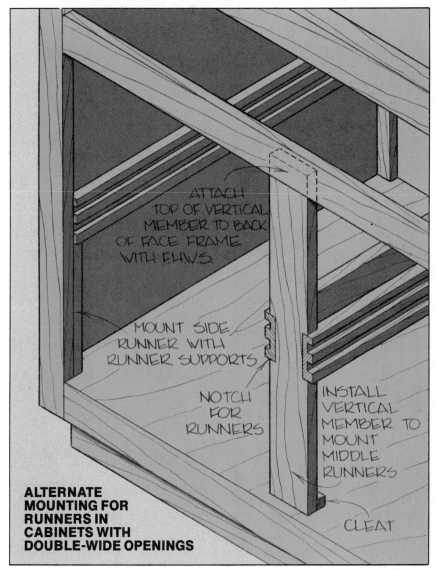

ATTACH TOP OF VERTICAL MEMBER TO BACK OF FACE FRAME WITH F.H.W.S.

MOUNT SIDE RUNNER WITH RUNNER SUPPORTS

NOTCH FOR RUNNERS

INSTALL VERTICAL MEMBER TO MOUNT MIDDLE RUNNERS

CLEAT

ALTERNATE MOUNTING FOR RUNNERS IN CABINETS WITH DOUBLE-WIDE OPENINGS

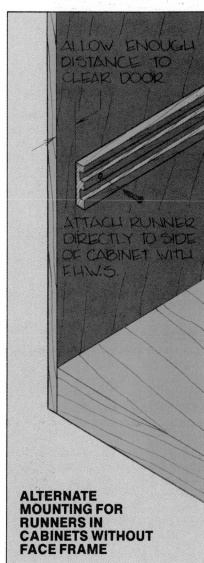

ALLOW ENOUGH DISTANCE TO CLEAR DOOR

ATTACH RUNNER DIRECTLY TO SIDE OF CABINET WITH F.H.W.S.

ALTERNATE MOUNTING FOR RUNNERS IN CABINETS WITHOUT FACE FRAME

9 Apply a finish to the bin and shelf.

To protect the wood and extend the life of the project, remove the bin and shelf from the cabinet and apply a waterproof, non-toxic finish. Use a penetrating oil, such as tung oil or salad bowl dressing. A finish that coats the wood will interfere with the sliding action. When the finish dries, fit the bin and the shelf back in the cabinet.

TRY THIS!   To help the bin and the shelf slide as smoothly as possible, rub the runners with paraffin.

Shadowbox Shelves

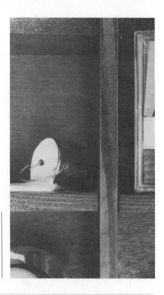

One of the most popular hobbies in this day and age is collecting miniatures. Is it any wonder? Look at all the miniatures available — boxes, automobiles, medals, doll furniture, toy soldiers, shells, rubber stamps — the list is endless. Even if you don't set out to collect one particular kind of miniature, most people gather tiny keepsakes. Many of us end up with a collection of miniatures without even trying to collect them.

Of course, once you have a few miniatures, you also have a miniature storage problem. How do you display these tiny treasures? Some people have found that old printer's *type cases* are the best solution. These cases had dozens of compartments for separating and organizing type in the days when each letter of the alphabet (and punctuation besides) was a separate piece. What makes these cases so wonderful is the variety of compartment sizes; a frequently-used letter had a big compartment, a seldom used one a small compartment. Upended, turned on their sides, and hung on a wall, these cases make tiny "shadowbox" shelves for miniatures.

Unfortunately, type cases are getting scarce. But they're easy to build; the shadowbox shelves

you see here are a reproduction of an old type case. They're easy to adapt, too. The overall dimensions of the shadowbox, the

arrangement of the partitions, and the size of the openings can all be customized to accommodate your personal collection. ✹

Materials List

FINISHED DIMENSIONS

PARTS

A.	Top/bottom (2)	½" x 2¼" x 21"
B.	Sides (2)	½" x 2¼" x 17"
C.	Back	¼" x 17½" x 20½"
D.	Long vertical dividers (5)	¼" x 2" x 17"
E.	Medium-long vertical divider	¼" x 2" x 10¼"
F.	Medium-short vertical divider	¼" x 2" x 8¾"
G.	Short vertical divider	¼" x 2" x 8"
H.	Long horizontal dividers (5)	¼" x 2" x 20"
J.	Short horizontal divider	¼" x 2" x 8¾"

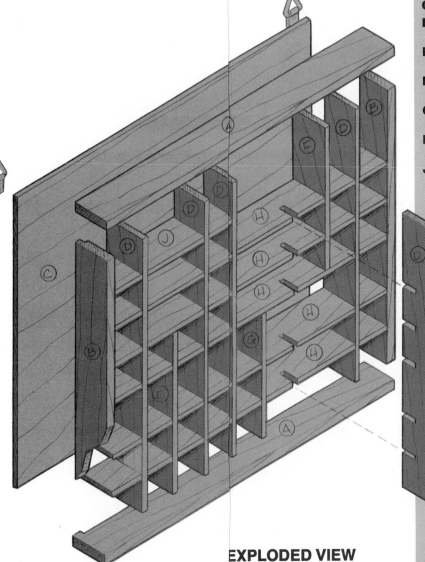

EXPLODED VIEW

HARDWARE

1" Brads (16-20)
Wall hangers (2)

1

Cut all parts to size. Plane solid stock to the thicknesses you'll need (¼″ and ½″) to make the top, bottom and dividers. Make the back from ¼″ plywood, or glue up stock edge-to-edge to make the width you need. Cut the parts to the sizes shown in the Materials List.

2

Cut the joinery in the frame parts.
The back is joined to the top, bottom and sides by ¼″-wide, ¼″-deep rabbets — regular rabbets in the sides and "double-blind" rabbets in the top and bottom. These double-blind rabbets are stopped on both the top and the bottom so that you don't see them when you assemble the frame.

Rout all of the rabbets with a straight bit or a rabbeting bit. Stop routing the double-blind rabbets before you cut through to the ends of the top and bottom; then square the corners of the rabbets with a chisel. (See Figure 1.) Dry assemble the frame parts to test the fit of the joints.

1/Stop routing the rabbets in the top and bottom before you cut through to the ends. Then square the corners of the rabbets with a hand chisel.

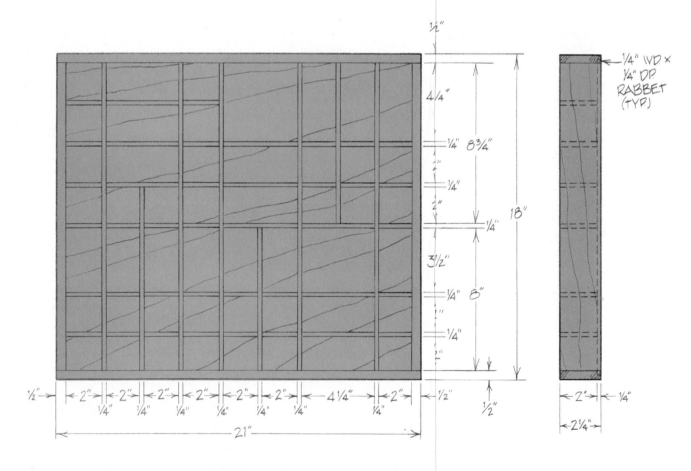

FRONT VIEW   **SIDE VIEW**

3

Cut the lap joints in the dividers.
Carefully lay out the lap joints on the dividers. Precision is important; if one joint is misplaced, it may ruin the fit of the entire assembly.

Mount a dado cutter on your table saw and set up to cut a dado ¼″ wide and 1″ deep. Also, attach a wooden extension to your miter gauge. Using this extension to guide your work, carefully cut the lap joints in the dividers.

After you've cut the joints, dry assemble the dividers to be sure they fit together properly.

TRY THIS! To help position the lap joints, use a stop block clamped to your miter gauge extension. For example, to cut all the lap joints that are 2″ away from the ends of a divider, secure the stop block to the extension 2″ away from the dado cutter. Then cut all the parts that need a lap in this position. To keep from cutting joints where you don't need them, carefully mark all the laps on all the parts *before* you start cutting.

4

Finish sand all parts. Scrape and sand the frame parts and the dividers, to get them ready to finish. Be careful not to remove too much stock from the dividers. If they are sanded too thin, the lap joints won't fit properly.

5

Assemble the shadowbox shelves.
Assemble the frame parts — top, bottom, sides, and back — with glue and brads. Put the horizontal and vertical dividers together with glue only. Remove any excess glue with a wet rag. Then glue the divider assembly in the frame assembly.

6

Finish the shelves. Finish sand any parts that still need it. Be careful to remove any glue beads with a chisel or a scraper.

Apply a finish to the completed project. We recommend that you use a simple, penetrating finish such as Danish oil or tung oil. There are too many nooks and crannies in this project to allow "rubbing out" a finish that builds on the surface of the wood, such as varnish or shellac. If you want the shelves to have a glossy look, apply several coats of tung oil. Mix the last coat with a little spar varnish.

When the finish dries, attach wall hangers to the back of the shelves. Hang the completed shadowbox on the wall as you would a picture frame.

TRY THIS! These small shelves seem to work best when they slant inward toward the wall slightly. This prevents tiny items from falling off. Glue two ¼″-thick spacers to the back of the shadowbox, near the bottom corners. These spacers will tip the shelves in the right direction.

Glass-Front Wall Cabinet

When you're looking around your home for additional storage space, consider the *walls*. A wall-hung storage unit, such as the glass-front cabinet shown here, makes use of the area *above* your furniture.

Cabinets such as this are deceptively easy to build and hang. While the glass-front unit looks elegant, it has no joint more complex than an ordinary dado or rabbet. It is hung on a beveled ledger strip that is screwed to the studs in the wall. Another beveled strip, attached to the back of the cabinet, interlocks with the wall-mounted ledger. These interlocking strips make it extremely easy to put the cabinet up — or take it down. And because the cabinet is supported along its entire length and attached directly to the frame of your house, you can store an enormous amount of weight in it.

This simple design is also very versatile. From this one set of plans, you can make many, many different wall-mounted cabinets. Change the height, width, or depth to fit the existing wall space. Apply different moldings, trim, or hardware to alter the style. Substitute solid or paneled doors if you don't want to see the contents of the cabinets. Or leave the doors off completely to make open shelves. Make whatever changes to the plan that you wish. It can be easily altered to fulfill a variety of storage needs.

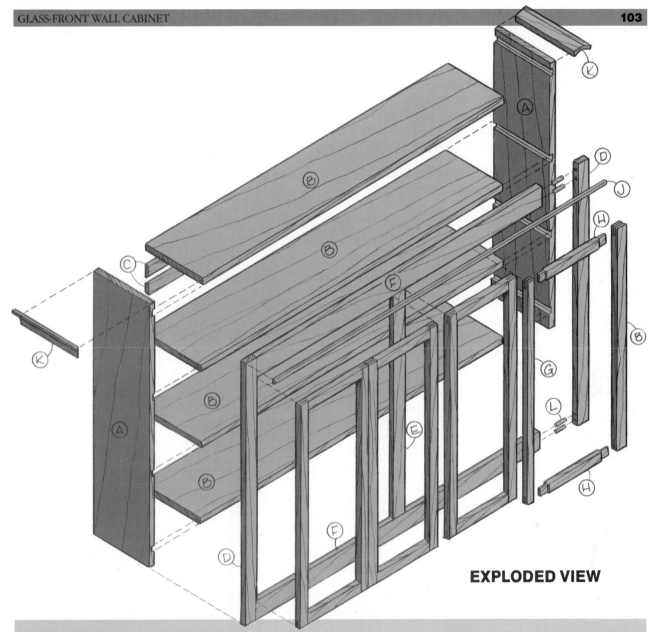

EXPLODED VIEW

Materials List

FINISHED DIMENSIONS

PARTS

A. Sides (2) ¾″ x 11″ x 42″
B. Shelves (4) ¾″ x 11″ x 57¾″
C. Ledger/mounting
strips (2) ¾″ x 2″ x 57″
D. Outside stiles (2) ¾″ x 2″ x 42″
E. Middle stile ¾″ x 2″ x 36″
F. Rails (2) ¾″ x 3″ x 54½″
G. Door stiles (8) ¾″ x 1½″ x 35⅞″
H. Door rails (8) ¾″ x 1½″ x 13″

J. Front molding ¾″ x 2⅝″ x 62¼″
K. Side
moldings (2) ¾″ x 2⅝″ x 13⅝″
L. Dowels (12) ⅜″ dia. x 2″

HARDWARE

1½″ x 2″ Brass butt hinges and
mounting screws (4 pairs)
Ring pulls and mounting screws (4)
Friction catches and mounting screws
  (4)
#10 x 1¼″ Flathead wood screws
  (24-30)
#10 x 1″ Flathead wood screws
  (10-12)
#14 x 3″ Flathead wood screws (3-4)
⅛″ x 10⅜″ x 33¼″ Glass panes (4)
Glazing points (24-32)

1

Adjust the size of the cabinet to fit your wall. Measure the space where you want to mount the cabinet, and adjust the design to fit this space. You can change the height, length, and depth of the cabinet simply by changing the dimensions of the parts of the case.

Caution: The cabinet that you see here is approximately 5′ wide. This is the maximum width for the cabinet *as designed.* If you make it any wider, the shelves may sag in the middle. To make a wider cabinet, you have to modify the design beyond simply changing the measurements. Divide the cabinet up into sections and add interior walls or "dividers" to help support the shelves every 3′ to 4′. Also, add a second ledger and mounting strip near the bottom of the case to help support the extra weight of a larger cabinet.

2

Cut the parts to size. To build this project as we have drawn it, purchase approximately 38 board feet of cabinet-grade lumber. If you change the dimensions, the amount of material will change, too. You can easily calculate the number of board feet you'll need by figuring the number of *square feet* of lumber you need and adding 10% extra for waste. Because all the flat parts are ¾″ thick (planed down from 1″-thick or "four-quarters" stock), the number of square feet will be equal to the number of board feet. (A board foot is 144 cubic inches of lumber.)

Once you have purchased the lumber and planed it to the proper thickness, cut all the parts to size *except* the moldings. Cut the stock to width, but leave it in one long strip until *after* you've shaped it.

When you make the ledger and mounting strip, rip a 45° bevel along one edge. As we show in *Section A,* these bevels interlock when you hang the cabinet.

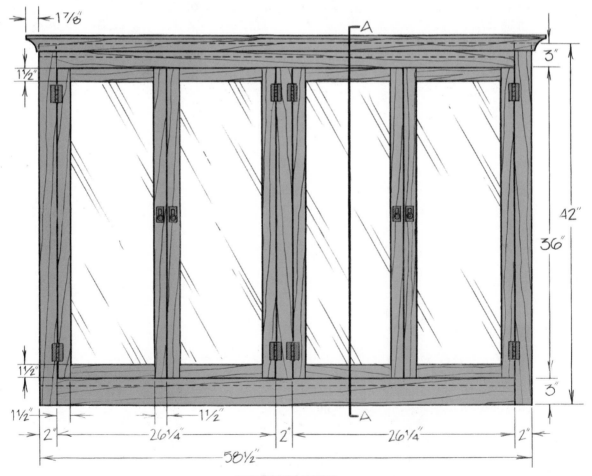

FRONT VIEW

3 **Cut the joinery in the sides.** Using a router or a dado cutter, make ¾″-wide, ⅜″-deep dadoes in the sides, as shown in the *Side Layout*. To save time and to ensure that you make both sides exactly the same, clamp the sides together, edge to edge. Cut the joinery in them both at the same time.

4 **Join the parts of the face frame.** Decide how you want to join the rails and stiles of the face frame. As we show in the *Exploded View,* these parts can be joined by dowels, but you can also use splines or biscuits. Make the joints, then assemble the parts to check their fit. Do not glue them together just yet.

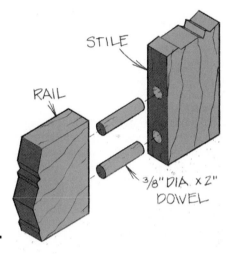

FACE FRAME JOINERY DETAIL

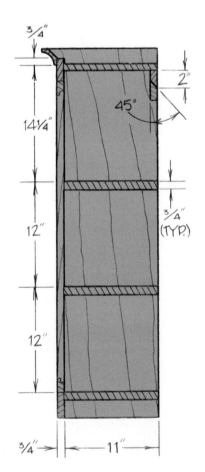

SECTION A

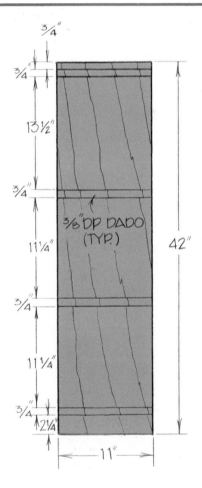

SIDE LAYOUT

5 Make the cove molding.

Make the cove molding in two steps: cutting the cove and chamfering the molding edges.

First, cut a cove in the face of the stock, using your table saw and an ordinary combination blade. Clamp a straightedge (to serve as a guide fence) to the saw table, angled at 30° to the blade. Adjust the depth of cut to just ⅛". Pass the molding stock over the blade at an angle, keeping one edge firmly against the straightedge. Readjust the depth of cut, raising the blade another ⅛", and make another pass. Repeat this process, cutting just ⅛" deeper with each pass until you have cut the cove ½" deep. (See Figures 1 and 2.)

Next, make the chamfers in the edges of the molding. You can do this with a table saw, but it's easier to do it on your jointer. Tilt the jointer fence at 45°, leaning in toward the knives. Adjust the depth of cut to ⁵⁄₃₂". Joint all four corners, making *two* passes over the knives to chamfer the *front* corners and *four* passes to chamfer the *back* corners. (See Figure 3.)

*1/*To cut the cove in the molding, first clamp a straightedge to the saw table as shown. The face of the straightedge should be 1¹⁵⁄₁₆" to the axis of the blade, so that cove will be cut in the center of the molding stock.

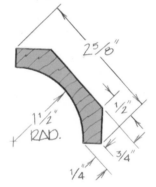

COVE MOLDING DETAIL

2⅝"
1½" RAD.
½"
¾"
¼"

*2/*Cut the cove in the molding by passing the wood across the saw blade at an angle. Make several passes, cutting just ⅛" deeper with each pass. On the last pass, feed the wood very *slowly,* so that the cut is as smooth as possible.

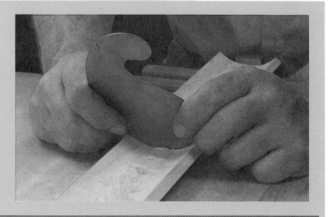

*3/*When you cut a chamfer with a jointer, also tilt the fence in toward *the* blade. This prevents the wood from slipping as you cut.

---

6 Finish sand all parts.

Finish sand all the parts that you have made so far, including the molding stock. Be careful not to round or "break" any edges or faces where two parts will be joined.

TRY THIS! To save time when smoothing the molding stock, use a "gooseneck" scraper to remove the saw marks from the cove. Turn the gooseneck until it fits the shape of the cove, then push it down and forward, holding the scraper so that it's tilted slightly forward.

7

Assemble the case. Dry assemble the sides, shelves, mounting strip, and the parts of the face frame to test their fit. Make any minor adjustments in the size and the shape of the parts to get a good fit, then disassemble the case.

Assemble the face frame, gluing the parts together. While the glue cures on the frame, assemble the sides, shelves, and mounting strip with glue and #10 x 1¼" flathead wood screws. To attach the shelves to the sides, drive the screws at an angle from the *inside* of the case, up through the bottom of the shelves and into the sides, as shown in the *Shelf-to-Side Joinery Detail.*

To attach the mounting strip to the sides/shelves assembly, first drill screw pockets at either end of the strip. Drive screws through the top shelf and into the square edge of the mounting strip. (The beveled edge of the strip must point down.) Then drive screws through the screw pockets to secure the ends of the mounting strip to the sides, as shown in the *Mounting Strip-to-Case Joinery Detail.* When the glue cures on both assemblies, glue the face frame to the sides and shelves.

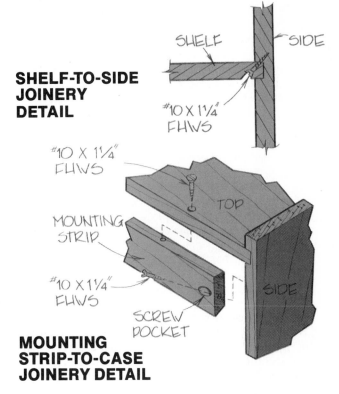

SHELF-TO-SIDE JOINERY DETAIL

MOUNTING STRIP-TO-CASE JOINERY DETAIL

8

Attach the molding to the case. Carefully fit the cove molding to the top of the case, mitering the ends where the front molding joins the side moldings. Attach the moldings with glue and #10 x 1" flathead wood screws. Drive the screws from inside the case, through the sides or face frame, and into the molding. This way, the screws won't show. (See Figure 4.)

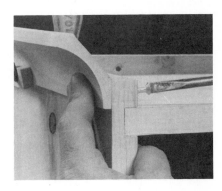

4/When you attach the moldings to the case, drive the screws with one hand and use the other hand to feel the front surface of the molding. If you feel the point of the screw beginning to come through the wood, stop immediately and substitute a shorter screw.

9

Assemble the door frames. Make the bridle joints (sometimes called slot or open mortises and tenons) that join the parts of the door frame. Using a tenon-cutting jig, make tenons in the ends of the door rails and mortises in the ends of the door stiles. (See Figure 5.) Assemble the door frames with glue, ensuring that the frames are absolutely square as you clamp them together.

Note: The door frame stock must be perfectly straight, with no twists, bends, warps, or other defects. *This is extremely important!* If the frame parts are even slightly distorted, the doors will not fit the case correctly.

When the glue dries on the door frames, rout the inside back of the frame, making a ¼"-wide, ¼"-deep

5/Use a tenon-cutting jig to cut both the mortises and the tenons of the bridle joints. The jig you see here can be easily made from scraps of wood. It rides along your table saw fence, guiding the wood over the blade.

rabbet all the way around the inside edge. Square the corners of this rabbet with a chisel. Finish sand the completed frames, removing all saw and mill marks.

10   ***Mount the doors in the case.***   Check the fit of the doors in the case. There should be a small gap (about 1/16″) between the door frames and the face frame all the way around the openings. There should also be a small gap between the adjacent doors. If the door seems too tight, use a block plane to remove a little stock from the door frame rails or stiles. When the doors fit to your satisfaction, attach them to the case with butt hinges. Mortise the hinges so that they are flush with the surfaces of the frames.

11   ***Install the pulls and catches.***   Mount ring pulls in the door frames, mortising them so that they are also flush with the surface of the wood. To keep the doors closed, install catches. Attach one part of each catch to the underside of the second-from-the-bottom shelf, and the other part to the back side of the door frame stiles.

12   ***Finish the completed wall cabinet.***   Remove the doors from the cabinet and remove all hardware. Do any touch-up sanding necessary to ready the project for finishing. Apply a finish to the case, door frames, and ledger strip. As you work, make certain to cover both the inside *and* the outside of the case equally. If you apply more coats of finish to one side of a board than you do to the other, that board will absorb moisture faster on one side where the finish is thin. In a short time it may warp or cup, ruining the project.

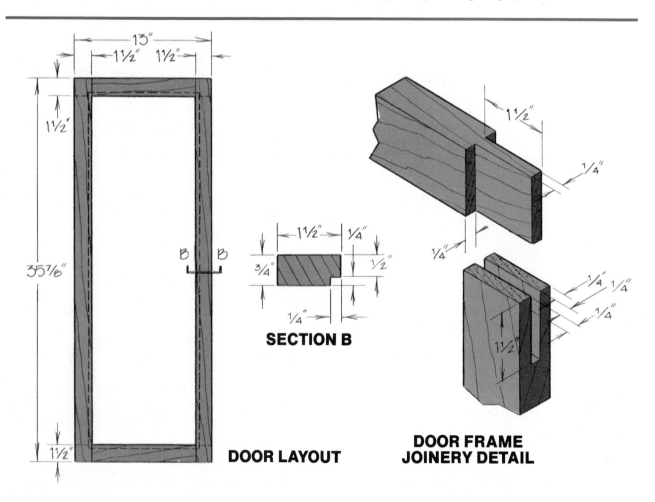

DOOR LAYOUT

SECTION B

**DOOR FRAME
JOINERY DETAIL**

13

Mount the cabinet on the wall. Using a measuring tape and a level, locate the position of the ledger strip on the wall, beveled side pointing up. Make sure that the ledger is perfectly horizontal. Attach the strip to the wall, driving #14 x 3″ screws through the strip and into the studs. *This is important!* The ledger must be attached directly to the studs in order to safely support the weight of the cabinet. When the ledger is secured, hang the cabinet, "hooking" the bevel of the mounting strip over the bevel of the ledger.

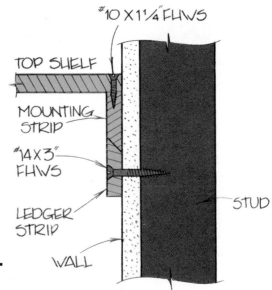

**LEDGER-TO-WALL
JOINERY DETAIL**

14

Install the glass in the doors. When the cabinet case is hung, replace the doors on the cabinet, and reattach all the hardware. Mount panes of glass in the doors, using glazing points to keep them in place. To keep the glass from rattling in the frames, put a small piece of felt between the glass and each glazing point.

Installing Hidden Screws

The screws that fasten the shelves to the sides in the glass-front wall cabinet are driven from inside the cabinet. Each screw is driven at an angle from the bottom side of the shelf up into the side. This makes the screw almost invisible when the cabinet is completely assembled.

Knowing how to hide screws is very useful. Professional cabinetmakers do it often when assembling both large and small cases. But it's also a bit tricky. You must drive the screws at just the right angle. If the angle is too steep or too shallow, the end of the screw will show.

To help install the screws at the correct angle, make yourself a drill guide from a scrap of hardwood. The guide should have *two* angled holes — a large hole for the counterbore and a smaller one for the pilot. Drill each screw hole in two steps — first the counterbore, then the pilot. Use stop collars on the bits to control the depth of the holes.

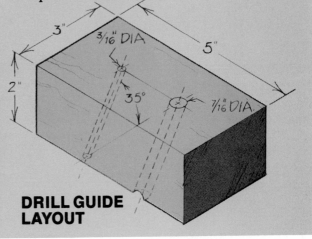

The drill guide keeps the bit at the proper angle, while the stop collar prevents it from boring too deeply.

**DRILL GUIDE
LAYOUT**

Diagonal Shelves

Shelves don't *have* to be horizontal. There are some advantages to making *diagonal* shelves — shelves that slope to one side or the other. The main advantage is that things that you place on diagonal shelves stay put. They slide down the shelf until they are stopped by another diagonal or divider. And there they sit, cradled securely in a "V" until you retrieve them. Piles of towels don't tumble down; rows of books don't lean on each other or fall over like so many drunks. Gravity keeps everything neat and tidy.

Diagonal shelves are normally built as standalone units or as inserts for larger storage units and closets. The shelves that you see here are typical.

The unit can sit alone on a counter, or it can be placed in a cabinet. Furthermore, it can rest on any side. The diagonal shelves will "work" no matter how the unit is placed.

Where the diagonals cross, they are joined by edge cross-lap (or just "edge-lap") joints, like dividers in an egg carton. The ends are mitered, and these are joined by dovetail-key joints. These dovetail keys not only reinforce the miter joints, they add a decorative touch. ●

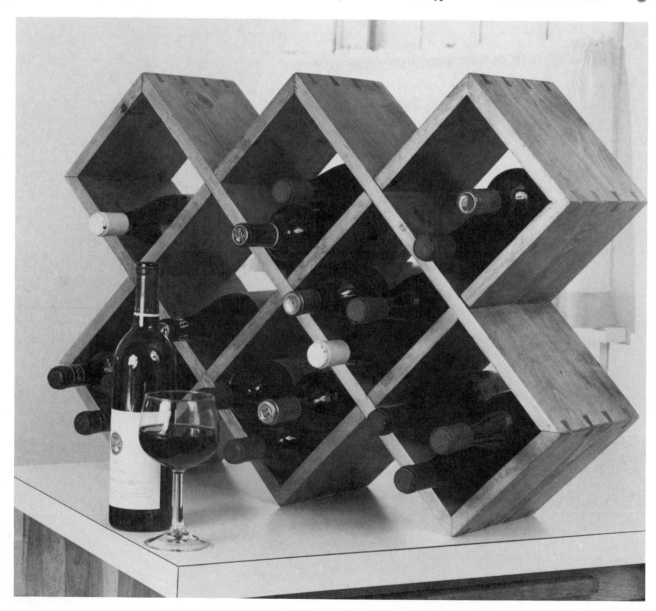

Materials List

FINISHED DIMENSIONS

PARTS

A. Long diagonals (2)   ¾″ x 8″ x 28¾″
B. Short diagonals (4)   ¾″ x 8″ x 21¾″
C. Ends (4)   ¾″ x 7¾″ x 8″
D. Dovetail keys (40)   ½″ x ½″ x 1″

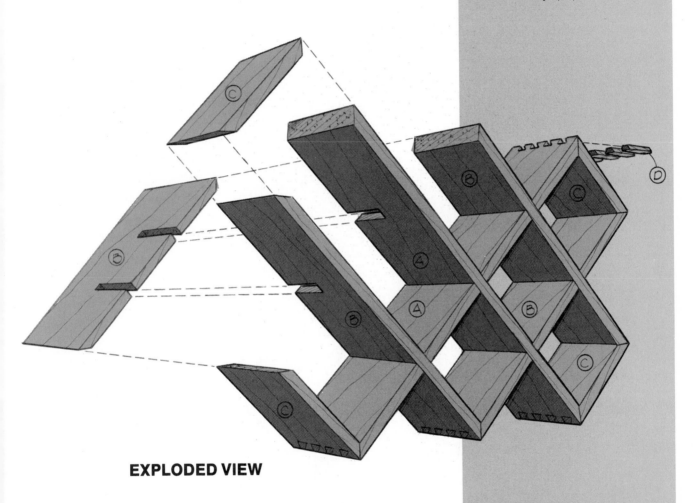

EXPLODED VIEW

1 Adjust the measurements to your needs.

As shown in the photograph, the diagonal shelves may be used as a wine rack. The measurements in the working drawings and the Materials List are figured from the average diameter and height of a wine bottle. If you build the shelves as drawn, each compartment will hold four bottles.

If you want to build these shelves to hold something other than wine, you will probably need to adjust the measurements. Compartments for books, for example, should be 12″ side to side and 10″ deep. Compartments for bath towels should be 14″ to a side and 9″ deep — depending on how you fold the towels. In addition to changing the size, you may also want to add or subtract compartments, making the shelving unit a different size *and* shape than what is shown here. But no matter how large the compartments are or how many of them you make, the construction will remain the same.

2 Cut all parts to size.

After you have adjusted the measurements of the units, select the lumber you need. To make the unit shown, you will need approximately 10 board feet of lumber. But this will change, of course, as you change the measurements. Choose *flat* stock — just as flat as you can find it. Any cup or twist in the boards will make the assembly of this project difficult.

Cut the parts to the sizes you need, and miter the ends of the boards as shown in the *Front View.* Note that the mitered ends of the ends and short diagonals all face the same direction — toward the "inside" — like the miters on the ends of picture frame members. But the mitered ends of the long diagonals face *opposite* directions.

> *TRY THIS!*   If you're making this project to hold towels or linens, build it from aromatic cedar. This will keep the cloth goods you put on the shelves smelling fresh.

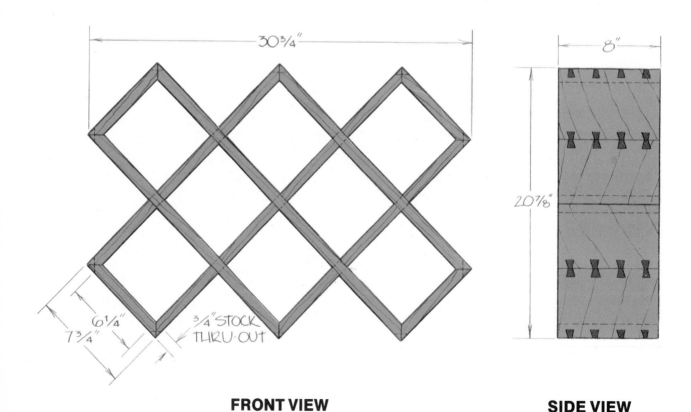

FRONT VIEW   **SIDE VIEW**

3 *Cut the edge lap joints in the diagonals.*

Carefully measure and mark the edge laps on *both* sides of the long and short diagonals. Using a table saw or a radial arm saw, just *start* to cut the sides of the lap joints. Finish the cuts with a back saw, then remove the waste with a chisel. (See Figure 1.) Because these joints are squared off at the bottom, you won't be able to cut them completely with a circular saw blade. By starting the cuts on a power saw, however, you save yourself a little work and make it easier to line up the back saw for a good, straight cut.

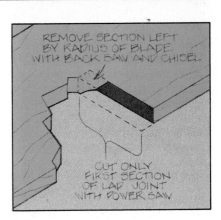

1/When you make the edge laps, start the cuts on your table saw or radial arm saw, sawing the shaded area in the illustration. Finish the cut (unshaded area) with a back saw, then remove the waste with a chisel.

4 *Finish sand all parts.* Dry assemble the parts (without glue) to be sure that they fit properly. When you're satisfied that they do, take them apart and finish sand all surfaces. As you sand, be careful not to round over the corners of adjoining surfaces.

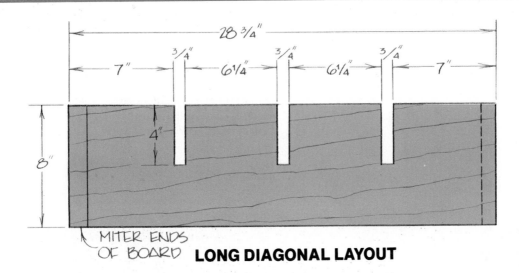

LONG DIAGONAL LAYOUT

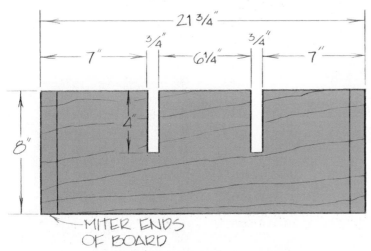

SHORT DIAGONAL LAYOUT

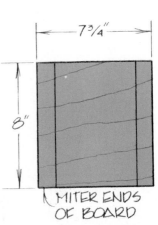

END LAYOUT

5

Assemble the shelving unit. Assemble the parts with glue, and wipe off any excess glue that squeezes out from between the joints with a damp rag. Use band clamps to hold the ends in place while the glue cures. (See Figure 2.) If you have miter clamps, use these to help align the corners where the short diagonals join each other. However, if you've used flat stock and have cut the edge laps accurately, the corners should align themselves with little need for clamping.

2/Use band clamps to hold the ends to the assembly while the glue dries. To prevent the band clamps from sticking to the miter joints where excess glue squeezes out, put a piece of masking tape over the joint.

6

Cut dovetail slots in the corners. To make dovetail key joints, first rout dovetail slots diagonally through the corners. From scraps of plywood, build a special "dovetail key joint jig" to guide the router. Refer to the *Dovetail Key Joint Jig/Exploded View* for the sizes of the parts and how they are assembled. Cut the parts to size, mitering the ends of the mounts and the braces. With a drill and a sabre saw, cut a slot in the worktable. Then attach the mounts and the braces to the

worktable with glue and screws. Finally, secure the guide to the worktable with screws *only*.

Note: Don't glue the guide in place. Being able to remove it makes the jig more versatile and allows you to cut key joints in a variety of projects, both large and small. Without the guide, you can use the jig on a router table to cut joints in small projects. With the guide, you can make joints in large projects, like the diagonal shelves.

After you've made the jig, place it over one corner of the shelving assembly, position it to cut the first slot, and clamp it to a diagonal. Mount a dovetail bit in the router, and adjust the height of the bit to cut a slot ⅝" deep. Slide the router across the jig, cutting the dovetail slot through the corner. Reposition the jig for the next slot and repeat. Continue until you have cut all the slots in all the corners. (See Figures 3 and 4.)

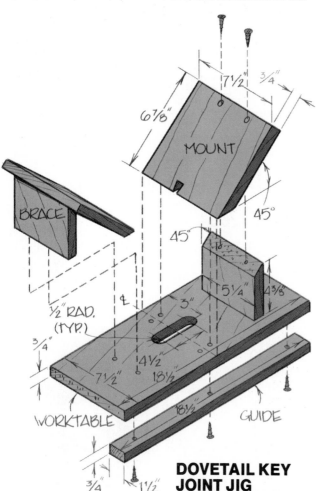

DOVETAIL KEY JOINT JIG EXPLODED VIEW

3/Use a special shop-made jig and a dovetail bit to rout the dovetail slots in the corners. Carefully adjust the depth of cut so that the router doesn't cut through to the inside surfaces of the shelves when you make the slots.

4/Cut several slots for dovetail keys in each corner. The spacing is not critical, but there should be enough keys to adequately reinforce the miter joint.

TRY THIS! The dovetail slots on the diagonal shelves that you see here are spaced 2″ apart. This spacing, however, is arbitrary. You can make them closer together or farther apart. You might also wish to space them randomly to give the joints the appearance of hand-crafted dovetails.

7 Insert dovetail keys in the slots.

Make the dovetail keys you need to fill the slots. The easiest way to make these keys is to use the same dovetail bit you used to rout the slots. Keep the bit mounted in your router, then mount the router under a router table. Clamp a fence to the table a short distance away from the bit.

Using this fence as a guide, cut one side of the key stock, then turn it over and cut the other. The two cuts will create a dovetail-shaped tenon along one edge of the board. (See Figure 5.) Rip this tenon from the board with a band saw or table saw, then cut it up into ¾″-long keys.

Glue these keys in the slots. (See Figure 6.) When the glue dries, sand the keys flush with the surface of the shelving assembly.

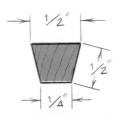

DOVETAIL KEY END VIEW

TRY THIS! The dovetail keys are decorative as well as functional, as previously noted. To make them more striking, cut them from a wood that *contrasts* with the wood you used to make the shelves. For example, if you made the shelves from light-colored birch or maple, use dark-colored walnut or mahogany for the keys.

5/To make the keys, use the dovetail router bit to cut a dovetail-shaped tenon along the edge of a board. Feed the board so that the rotation of the bit helps to hold it against the fence. After you've made the tenon, rip it from the board.

6/Glue the keys in the slots. After the glue dries, cut the protruding parts of the keys off with a dovetail saw and sand them flush with the surface of the wood.

8 Finish the completed shelving unit.

Do any necessary touch-up sanding on the completed shelves, then apply a finish. If you use a stain and you *don't* want the dovetail keys to be darker than the surrounding wood, coat the ends of the keys with a sanding sealer *before* applying the stain. Otherwise, the stain will soak into the end grain of the keys, darkening them faster than the surrounding face grain.

Audio Rack

Every audiophile faces the same storage problems. First of all, how do you organize your audio components — the amplifiers, mixers, tape players, compact disc players, and on and on? This problem is compounded because many of us purchase several different brands of equipment, either to get a good buy or the best component for the money. Many off-the-shelf audio racks are made to hold just one manufacturer's equipment.

Secondly, if you use a bookcase or a cabinet, how do you dissipate the heat that electronic equipment produces? If the case isn't properly ventilated, the heat will build up, damaging the components. Most wooden cases have air holes in the back, but this does not provide adequate ventilation if you have more than two or three components.

Finally, how do you organize the myriads of wires that you need to hook together a good sound system? Not only do most components have a power cord, there are speaker wires, antennas, and cables that run between the components. If not stowed properly, these wires will not only detract from the appearance of your sound system, they may cause a hazard.

The rack you see here solves all of these problems. The shelves are adjustable, and the dimensions are calculated to accept standard-sized (19″ wide) audio components. The project will store most of the equipment made by the better manufacturers. The rack has an open design, so the equipment will be properly ventilated, no matter how many components you stack together. And the rack has a unique false back, a compartment running the entire length of the project, with hooks and cleats to organize the wires, and a power strip so that you can plug in all the equipment. The only wires that need to hang out of the rack are the speaker wires and a single power cord.

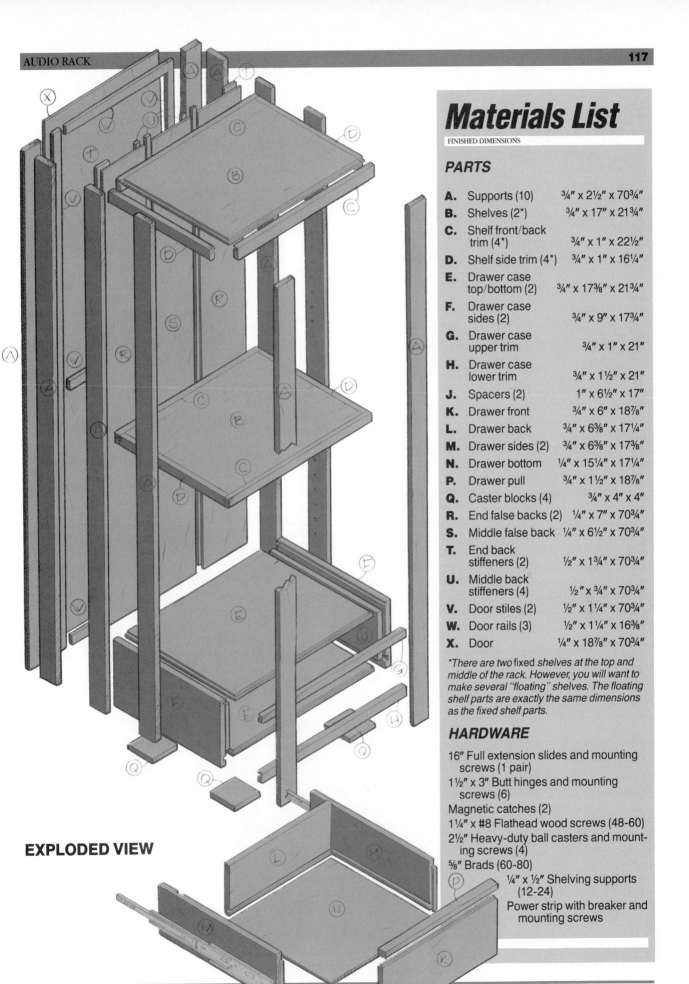

EXPLODED VIEW

Materials List

FINISHED DIMENSIONS

PARTS

A. Supports (10)   ¾" x 2½" x 70¾"

B. Shelves (2*)   ¾" x 17" x 21¾"

C. Shelf front/back trim (4*)   ¾" x 1" x 22½"

D. Shelf side trim (4*)   ¾" x 1" x 16¼"

E. Drawer case top/bottom (2)   ¾" x 17⅜" x 21¾"

F. Drawer case sides (2)   ¾" x 9" x 17¾"

G. Drawer case upper trim   ¾" x 1" x 21"

H. Drawer case lower trim   ¾" x 1½" x 21"

J. Spacers (2)   1" x 6½" x 17"

K. Drawer front   ¾" x 6" x 18⅞"

L. Drawer back   ¾" x 6⅜" x 17¼"

M. Drawer sides (2)   ¾" x 6⅜" x 17⅜"

N. Drawer bottom   ¼" x 15¼" x 17¼"

P. Drawer pull   ¾" x 1½" x 18⅞"

Q. Caster blocks (4)   ¾" x 4" x 4"

R. End false backs (2)   ¼" x 7" x 70¾"

S. Middle false back   ¼" x 6½" x 70¾"

T. End back stiffeners (2)   ½" x 1¾" x 70¾"

U. Middle back stiffeners (4)   ½" x ¾" x 70¾"

V. Door stiles (2)   ½" x 1¼" x 70¾"

W. Door rails (3)   ½" x 1¼" x 16⅜"

X. Door   ¼" x 18⅞" x 70¾"

There are two fixed shelves at the top and middle of the rack. However, you will want to make several "floating" shelves. The floating shelf parts are exactly the same dimensions as the fixed shelf parts.

HARDWARE

16" Full extension slides and mounting screws (1 pair)

1½" x 3" Butt hinges and mounting screws (6)

Magnetic catches (2)

1¼" x #8 Flathead wood screws (48-60)

2½" Heavy-duty ball casters and mounting screws (4)

⅝" Brads (60-80)

¼" x ½" Shelving supports (12-24)

Power strip with breaker and mounting screws

1 ***Cut all parts to size.*** Before you purchase the wood or hardware for this project, check your audio components and make sure they will fit in the rack. The rack is designed to hold most standard-sized components, so chances are yours will fit just fine. But it pays to be sure.

Once you are sure that your equipment will fit, and you've made any adjustments to the design that are necessary, purchase the materials. You'll need approximately 30 board feet of ¾″-thick stock, one-half to one full sheet of ¾″ plywood (depending on how many shelves you make), a full sheet of ¼″ plywood, and the hardware listed in the Materials List.

When you've gathered the materials, cut all the wooden parts to the sizes shown. You may have to adjust the size of the drawer parts somewhat, depending on the extension slides you purchased. As designed, the drawer will work with ½″-wide slides. If your slides are narrower or fatter, adjust the size of the drawer back and drawer bottom accordingly.

2 ***Assemble the shelves and drawer case.*** Using a router or a dado cutter, cut ¼″-wide, ⅜″-deep grooves in the inside face of the shelf trim parts, drawer case trim parts, and drawer case sides. Cut matching tongues in the edges of the shelves and drawer case top and bottom, using the same tools. (See Figure 1.) While you set up to cut these joints, also cut the groove in the drawer pull and the tongue in the drawer front. Set these parts aside until later.

Check the fit of the parts. When you're satisfied that the shelving and drawer case parts fit together properly, glue the trim to the shelves. Glue *and* screw the spacers to the inside faces of the drawer case sides. Then assemble the rest of the drawer case with glue only. Check that the drawer case is square as you clamp the parts together.

Note: The end grain of some of the trim parts will be visible when you assemble the shelves and the drawer case. Do not be concerned about this. The end grain will be hidden by the corner supports when you complete the project.

1/Using a dado cutter mounted to your table saw, cut the tongues in the edges of the shelves, drawer case top and bottom, and drawer front.

SHELF MOLDING JOINERY DETAIL

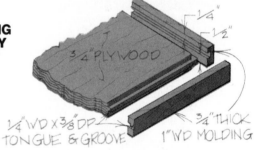

¾″ PLYWOOD

¼″ WD × ⅜″ DP TONGUE & GROOVE

¾″ THICK 1″ WD MOLDING

¼″

1½″

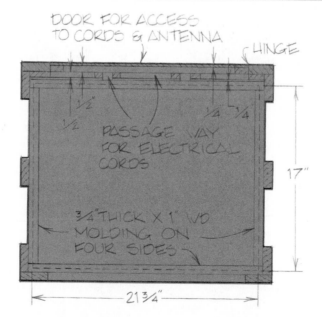

DOOR FOR ACCESS TO CORDS & ANTENNA

HINGE

½″

½″

¼″ ¾″

PASSAGE WAY FOR ELECTRICAL CORDS

17″

¾″ THICK × 1″ WD MOLDING ON FOUR SIDES

21¾″

SECTION A

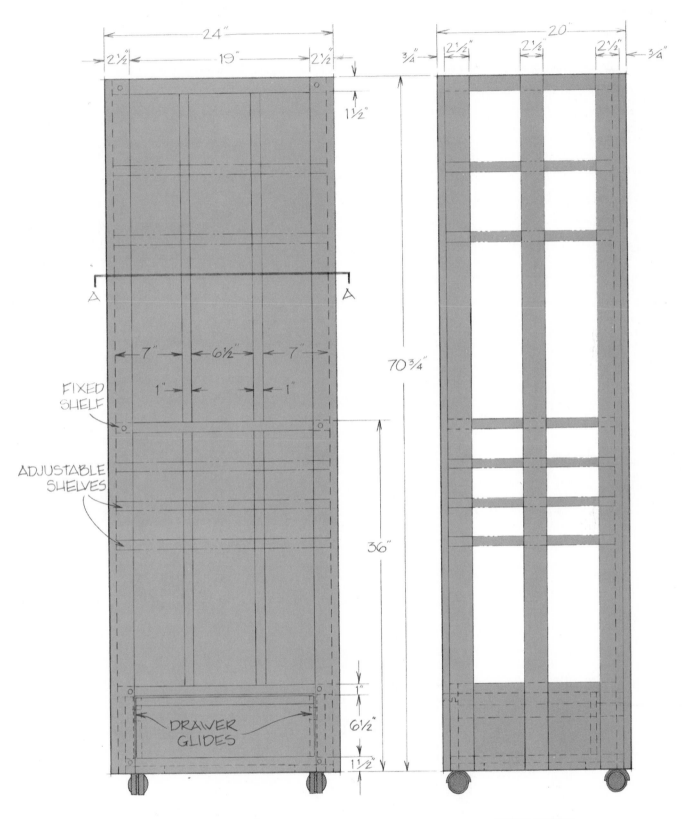

FRONT VIEW

SIDE VIEW

3

Drill the shelf support holes in the supports. Mark the locations of the shelving support holes on the four side corner supports, as shown in the *Corner Support Layout*. Drill ¼″-diameter, ⅜″-deep stopped holes where you have marked the stock.

TRY THIS! There are a lot of holes to drill, and you can save time by setting up a jig to help drill them all. Attach a fence to your drill press to automatically position the holes side-to-side in the stock, and use a "stop" to automatically space the holes.

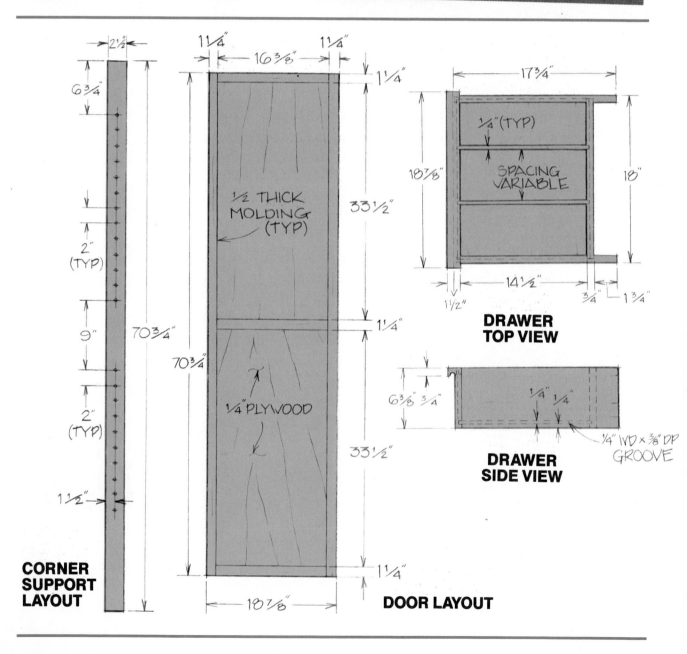

CORNER SUPPORT LAYOUT

2½″ · 6¾″ · 2″ (TYP) · 9″ · 70¾″ · 2″ (TYP) · 1½″

DOOR LAYOUT

1¼″ · 16⅜″ · 1¼″ · 1¼″ · 33½″ · ½ THICK MOLDING (TYP) · 1¼″ · 70¾″ · ¼″ PLYWOOD · 33½″ · 1¼″ · 18⅞″

DRAWER TOP VIEW

17¾″ · ¼″ (TYP) · SPACING VARIABLE · 18⅞″ · 18″ · 14½″ · ¾″ · 1¾″ · 1½″

DRAWER SIDE VIEW

6⅜″ · ¾″ · ¼″ · ¼″ · ¼″ WD × ⅜″ DP GROOVE

4

Assemble the false backs and the door. Glue the stiffeners to the false backs. Also, glue the rails and stiles to the door where shown in the *Door Layout*. Reinforce the glue joints on the door with brads.

5

Assemble the audio rack. Finish sand all the parts that need it — shelves, supports, drawer case, and false backs. (Set the door aside for the time being.) Assemble the corner supports with glue and screws. Counterbore and countersink the screws, then cover the screw heads with wooden plugs.

When the glue dries, *dry assemble* the rack with *screws only*. Be sure to leave a 1″ space between the false backs, to create a passageway for the electrical cords and wires.

Don't glue any more parts together at this point, just check the fit of the parts and assemblies you've already made. You'll need a helper or two to put all these parts together; don't try to do it by yourself unless you've got a *lot* of clamps — or eight arms.

When you're satisfied with the fit of the parts you've made, reassemble the rack with glue *and* screws. Once again, counterbore and countersink the screws, then cover the screw heads with wooden plugs.

6

Assemble and mount the drawer. Cut the drawer joinery with a router. Rout sliding dovetail joints to hold the sides to the front, as shown in the *Drawer Front Joinery Detail*. (See also Figures 2 and 3.) Rout dadoes to attach the back to the sides. Also, make grooves on the inside faces of the drawer parts to hold the bottom. If you wish, you can also make dadoes to insert dividers in the drawer, to help organize your cassettes and compact disks. Finally, rout a cove in the underside of the drawer pull with a veining bit.

Dry assemble the drawer to check the fit of the parts. If they fit properly, reassemble the parts with glue. Make sure the drawer is square when you clamp the parts together.

To mount the drawers in the drawer case, disassemble the extension slides. Most extension slides have two components — the slide and the mount. (See Figure 4.) Attach the slides to the spacers inside the case and the mounts to the sides of the drawer. Measure carefully where you want to put the mounts — they have to be placed precisely so that the drawer will be properly positioned in the case. Install the drawer in the case by fitting the mounts in the slides.

2/To make a sliding dovetail joint, first rout a groove with a dovetail bit. A router table with a fence helps to guide the cut.

3/Then make a tenon that matches the groove. Leave the dovetail bit positioned for the same depth-of-cut, and move the fence closer to the bit. Pass the board in between the bit and the fence, turn the board over, and make another pass.

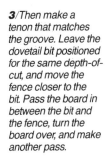

4/The extension slides come apart into two pieces to make it easy for you to install them. Attach the slides to the spacers inside the drawer case and the mounts to the drawer sides.

DRAWER FRONT JOINERY DETAIL

DRAWER PULL

SIDE

¼″ WD X ⅜″ DP TONGUE & GROOVE

FRONT

SLIDING DOVETAIL

7 **Mount the audio rack on casters.** Attach the caster blocks to the bottom of the drawer case with glue and screws. Then mount ball casters on the caster blocks.

8 **Mount the door on the audio rack.** Put the door in place on the back of the audio rack and check the fit. If it binds, remove a little stock where the door rubs on the supports with a block plane and sandpaper. When the door fits properly, mount it on the right back support with butt hinges. Install magnetic catches to keep the door closed.

9 **Install the floating shelves.** Put shelving supports in the holes in the corner supports where you want to suspend a shelf, then put the shelves in place on the supports. (See Figure 5.) You may have to remove a little stock from the edges of the shelves so that they fit in the rack without binding.

5/Each shelf rests on four "shelving supports," which are installed in the holes in the corner supports. These shelving supports can be rearranged in their holes to change the levels of the shelves according to your needs.

10 **Finish the audio rack.** Disassemble all the hardware from the rack — hinges, catches, casters, and extension slides. Do any touch-up sanding that needs to be done, and apply a finish. When the finish dries, reassemble the rack.

TRY THIS! Rather than plugging all your components into separate power outlets, install a single "power strip" behind the false backs, as shown. Rout the power cords through the gaps between the false backs and plug them into this power strip. Run a single cord from the power strip to a wall outlet.

Credits

Contributing Craftsmen and Craftswomen:

Larry Callahan (Audio Rack)

Nick Engler (Bracket Shelves, Adjustable Bookcase, Super-Quick Shelves, Glass-Front Wall Cabinet, Slide-Out Bins and Shelves, Wall Units, Peg-Rail Storage Units, Diagonal Shelves, Classic Television Stand)

Mary Jane Favorite (Diagonal Shelves, Shadowbox Shelves)

Rich Fritz (Stacking Boxes, Bicycle Rack)

Phil Gehret (Closet Organizers)

Fred Matlack (Blanket Chest, Firewood Box, Stacking Boxes, Bicycle Rack)

The designs for the projects in this book are the copyrighted property of the craftsmen and craftswomen who built them. Readers are encouraged to reproduce these projects for their personal use or for gifts. However, reproduction for sale or profit is forbidden by law.

Special Thanks To:

C&J Party Supply, West Milton, Ohio

Christmas Barn, Bethlehem, Pa.

Country Junction, Emmaus, Pa.

Curtain Concepts, Allentown, Pa.

Donegal Square, Bethlehem, Pa.

Julie's Sewing Basket, Emmaus, Pa.

The Studebaker Family Homestead, Tipp City, Ohio

Wertz Hardware Stores, West Milton, Ohio

Dan and Pauline Campanelli, Warren County, N.J.

Marianne Laubach